CHASING YOUR LIFE

A Spiritual Journey from Stress
to Success (and Peace)

JOSEPH NUNZIATA

Motivational PRESS
LEADERS IN GLOBAL PUBLISHING

Published by Motivational Press, Inc.
1777 Aurora Road
Melbourne, Florida, 32935
www.MotivationalPress.com

Manufactured in the United States of America.

ISBN: 978-1-62865-483-7

CONTENTS

This book is dedicated to my father Joseph Nicholas Nunziata whose personal chase helped me see the pain and suffering attached to this phenomenon. His journey will now help others avoid this pain and create more peaceful lives.

To my son, Eric who instinctively lives in a state of flow, ease, and trust. He showed me what it looks like to live a life I did not think possible.

To my beautiful wife, Maria who gave me unconditional love and support. She helped me see the possibilities and power of true love.

FOREWORD

I FEEL MY FATHER ASKED ME to write the forward to this book because I have always beaten to my own drum, regardless of societal and cultural expectations. The world teaches the importance of "chasing" your dreams, yet this is a fallacy. Chasing anything is often times not ideal. For example, if you were to start chasing someone down the street, running as fast as you can, what would happen? The person would sprint in the opposite direction.

Life is somewhat like this person on the street. When we are focused on the outcome of certain events, it takes us out of the moment and away from the actual journey. We lose an element of genuine enjoyment and happiness. That is why it is important not to chase after goals. It is important to have goals and aspirations, yet instead of chasing them, it is more constructive to set your intentions towards what you want. Sometimes this requires action, and other times it is imperative to wait and prepare YOURSELF for what is to come. Everything is always working for our benefit even when this is not visible to us. Each and every one of us has the ability to create positivity and love in our lives, yet it is not always about chasing these things down. Chasing things can be unpleasant, and is often less effective.

I urge you to wake up every morning with the intention to be your most genuine self, and to be a positive force on the people around you. This is a true state of flowing. When you are in a state of flow, you are not stressed, nor are you worried about the outcome. Instead you are living life to the fullest. Positivity and opportunity often arise as a result of implementing this philosophy.

The teachings and lessons given to me at a young age have shaped my view to be different than that of tradition. I have found when you try to work hard to meet the expectations of others, you are making everyone happy except for yourself. In all honesty, even those who impose these expectations on you aren't happy either. We are each given the gift of life, it is too precious to waste trying to satisfy everyone outside of yourself. Each of us is put on this Earth as an amazing individual, as unique and spectacular as nature itself and it is the right of every individual to live their life to the fullest. The beauty is, a full, happy life takes a different form for everyone, and there isn't a single thing wrong with that.

Have you ever said something like this to yourself? "WOW! No matter WHAT I do I keep getting a disappointing result!" Whether it be our career, our love life, our health or our family, it seems that universally we have all had this experience at some point or another in our lives. Living with the feeling that no matter what you do you cannot make things the way you want, or at least change things for the better. Constantly chasing after goals that for some reason seem to be out of reach.

From the moment we are born we are influenced by the people and world around us. Many people you meet will tell you "the way the world works" based on their perception of life. People say things like "Chase your dreams!" and "I'll sleep when I'm dead" implying there is so much work to be done there isn't even time to rest. Hard work is important, yet so is leading a balanced life. The multitude of outside opinions we are constantly subjected to often dictate not only the way we view the world, but the way we view ourselves and approach our everyday lives. Not only does this mentality not work, it can be detrimental to an individual's mental and emotional state. Why is it that so many of us find ourselves pushing so hard to no avail?

The reason for this is because society teaches us the importance of hard work and determination while excluding other essential information. Imagine you are working on a puzzle and only have access to half of the pieces. Although you would manage to put some of the pieces together, you will never get the whole picture. We work on our external goals without ever stopping and taking the time to work on OURSELVES.

We approach life and work hard and push for things that may not even be right for us, and when the result is not what we desired we are disappointed. We are approaching things backwards. First, we must look inward before we look outside of ourselves. Self-awareness and emotional intelligence are the other half of the puzzle. *Chasing Your Life* is here to provide you with the missing pieces of the puzzle; and to show you how to approach life in a way that creates positivity and love in all facets.

It is up to you to make the choice to put the pieces together and create the picture you want for your life. The journey will not always be easy, but the results you will create will be worth it. The first step in healing the world is for everyone to first heal themselves. Happiness and success are on the horizon, all you have to do is be courageous enough to take the first step.

Eric Nunziata

Spiritual Warrior

INTRODUCTION

WE SEEM TO SPEND OUR lives here on earth chasing something we believe will make us happy. It may be fame or fortune, the person you love, a job title or level of status. Unfortunately, many people leave this world with a sense of failure and longing, as we tend to focus on what we did not achieve or acquire in this life. This external chase has been the cause of so much pain and suffering for many.

On the other hand, our desire to create and improve has helped us advance in many ways. We have moved from caves to homes with heat, running water and refrigerators filled with food. We have seen amazing technological breakthroughs, but have we advanced emotionally and spiritually? Are we still chasing peace and happiness in the form of external possessions and false identities?

There is a delicate balance between moving forward and stepping back. Knowing when to act and when to sit still is the key to creating a more flowing life. This book will explore this delicate balance and help you make the decisions that are best for your soul's unique journey. You will discover the keys to feeling peaceful, relaxed and flowing.

» Why do we chase?

» And what are we chasing?

It is a riddle as old as human existence and it is what makes us humans so wonderful. Learning to eliminate the chase is the key to creating a successful, peaceful and joyful life here on earth. Human beings have an innate desire to feel love and improve; these are the desires that trigger the chase. Now it is time to reframe our lives, stop chasing and create balance.

This book is dedicated to bringing this phenomenon to light. It will help you understand why you do the things you do.

Much of our chasing nature was created by what we learned at home and in society. We have been conditioned to believe that when we attain a certain level of success or accumulate enough external possessions we will be happy. This can be anything from a new car, to fame and adulation from adoring fans. In the end, all external accomplishments, no matter how great, are fleeting. They will not give you the peace and fulfillment your soul truly desires.

I am not suggesting you give up on your dreams or desire to accomplish things in your life. We are here to create and share our gifts with the world. This desire to create drives us forward. In some cases this drive to succeed can take over your life and cause you to lose balance.

If you want to become more peaceful you must stop chasing these dreams and desires. This may sound terrific or horrifying, depending on your perspective, but stopping is more difficult than you can imagine. You have been trained and conditioned to chase what you desire. It is in your DNA. When you stop, you lose your sense of purpose and identity.

There is a delicate balance to be attained here. You will always desire more, which is fine, but you must learn to live in a state of complete acceptance. Achieving this feat, and yes it is a feat, will challenge you on every level.

You must also accept that what you seek in the external world is a moving target. Nothing stays the same and each accomplishment dissolves as soon as you attain it. Then we are on to the next item on the list.

- » What if there was no list?
- » What if there was nothing to accomplish?
- » What if your entire focus was on sharing your gifts with world?
- » How would your life change if all you focused on was sharing and peace?

Join me as we explore a new way to live your life here on earth. I will warn you that this new path is much more peaceful and rewarding. If that is your desire, this is the book for you.

WHAT ARE YOU
REALLY CHASING?

1

TO TRULY UNDERSTAND YOURSELF it is important to go back to the beginning and identify the essence of your chase. Your short life here on earth is designed for your unique emotional experience. You are here to feel the full spectrum of emotions at the highest level.

Emotions come in two basic flavors; we would describe them as positive or negative. You either feel good or bad, happy, or sad, peaceful, or disturbed, you get the picture. In this world of opposites or, yin and yang, we need both sides to create a full experience. You would not know the feeling of joy without the feeling of sadness. These, so called negative feelings, are a very important part of our human experience.

Ultimately, we all want to feel love. This is the most powerful feeling in the universe and it is the emotion we are really chasing. I could end this book right now because you know you are chasing the feeling of love. The issue is, understanding the origin of your chase and then stopping it.

The question: Why are you chasing love and why can't you seem to find it?

The answer: You are looking in the wrong place.

The reason you are as the song says "looking for love in all the wrong places" is based on multiple factors including your beliefs, DNA, mission here on earth and the desire to receive love from your parents. When you were born, you were a perfect expression of love.

As human beings, we seek love and attention from the most important figures in our lives...our parents. When we do not receive the amount of love required we spend our lives chasing it. Just for the record, no matter how wonderful your parents were they will fall short here. It is impossible to give your child all the love they desire. This is what the human experience is all about. We come here to find it ourselves and reconnect to source. Each person is traveling along their own version of the *Yellow Brick Road.*

In the Wizard of Oz, Dorothy goes on an amazing journey. Her quest is all about getting home. She believes the Wizard has the answer she seeks. In the end, the Good Witch of the North tells her, *"You've always had the power."* We are on the exact same journey. Reaching a point when you know and believe the power is within you.

Everyone suffers from the feeling of not enough love, on some level. It does not matter how much love you received or did not receive, no one is 100% fulfilled. This is not meant to judge your parents. As a parent, I accept that I did not give my son all the love he required. Your parents,' gave you the amount of love and attention they were capable of giving. It was simply not enough to make you feel whole. Thus, you go out and attempt to fill in the blanks in other places. Seeking this feeling is at the core of each person's journey and chase.

There are many places to seek the feeling of love:

» Your relationships

» Your job

» Your accomplishments

» Your possessions

» Your physical body

» Your family

As a child, you know you want this feeling of love but you don't seem to be receiving enough of it. You begin to seek answers and solutions to the problem. I see it likes gears turning in your head. These gears move faster and faster in a desperate attempt to find the answer and solve the problem.

All your trouble begins with a simple thought.

They will love me when I...

» Have a perfect report card

» Make the team

» Win an award

» Take care of my younger siblings

» Get a job

» Get married

» Have children

» Become successful

When you reach the first milestone and the feeling of love is still missing, your mind moves on to the next item on the list. Oh, I will receive the love when I (fill in the blank).

Your mind gets in the way here because it is designed to solve problems. If plan A did not work you move on to plan B.

This creates tremendous frustration for your mind which is desperately trying to solve the problem. The bad news, there is no mental or logical solution to this problem. You have now become trapped in an endless cycle of chasing.

One of the first steps in this process is getting out of your head. This is not easy because you have been trained to use your mind to survive. The idea of abandoning it seems counterintuitive.

As you grow up, the chase continues with people outside your family. If I am not receiving this love from my family I will seek it elsewhere. Now you have expanded the circle in a desperate attempt to find the love you seek.

Maybe my teacher, my boss, my friends, my co-workers, my boyfriend or girlfriend will give me these amazing feelings I never received at home. This type of thinking puts tremendous pressure on every other person and situation in your life. It also creates expectations from others that can never be met.

Many people believe that a good relationship is the answer to their problems. In this example an expectation was created regarding the person you are going to meet. This person has now become the answer which adds tremendous pressure to building a relationship. This is a case of seeking the love outside of yourself.

Now you know you are chasing love from the outside world. Looking at this from a mental perspective, you may believe this behavior will be easy to stop. Being aware is the first step to making the changes you seek. Knowing something is great but it is only a small piece of the puzzle, changing your internal feelings and creating new results is a bit more involved. You must work on your inner-self to make the changes you desire.

Becoming aware of something moves you into the light. This is how we begin the process of enlightenment. Expanded awareness gives you a new perspective and different view of the situation. The situation has not changed but your view is now completely different.

I like to use this example when describing perspective. Let's say you were at the Empire State Building in New York City. If you are standing at the bottom you would have a limited view. You would see people walking, stores, vendors, and traffic in the street. When you ascend to the top of the building you are now 102 stories above the street. Your perspective is now completely different. You can see for miles and on a clear day they say you can see five different states. The interesting thing is, you are in the exact same place. The only difference is you are now seeing things from a higher perspective.

As you elevate your awareness you are no longer reacting to the situation in front of you. On a higher level, you realize there is something else going on here. You are having an emotional experience to help your soul grow. This new perspective will completely change the way you deal with life and make decisions.

YOUR DECISION-MAKING PROCESS

Every day people get out of bed and make a series choices. Some of these decisions are mundane while others can be life-changing. The reasons why you make certain decisions and how they impact your life is very important.

When you are holding yourself in pain you are making choices that impact you in a negative way. Why would you do that? It makes absolutely no sense at all. This is where the problem begins.

We look to the mind and believe once we know something we can change it. This belief is the negative ego's best friend.

Weight loss is a great example because it is so prevalent in our society. It is also something visible for the world to see. You could be an alcoholic and hide it for years. When I was in my twenties I worked as a bartender in New York City. Every day respectable looking people in business attire would come in during lunch and after work to have drinks. I remember thinking, how are these people able to get up every day and function at work. There are millions of people living in this condition. They are masking their pain and most people never know it. Eventually this abuse breaks people down and creates serious issues.

There is no hiding your weight. Your physical appearance is out there for the world to see and judge. I could walk up to any person in the world and ask, *"What do I have to do to lose weight?"* They would all respond in pretty much the same way. *"You have to eat less and exercise more."* That sounds so simple. It sounds simple because at the core it is simple.

We have now solved the obesity problem for the entire planet with one simple concept, *Eat Less, Exercise More.* The question is this, if everyone knows the answer why aren't they doing it? They are not doing it because it is not about knowledge. This is a common theme with addiction. Addicts know their behavior is destructive to themselves and many others but they can't seem to stop.

Knowledge and awareness is only the first step in your transformational process. It is an important step, but it is only the beginning. Now you are aware. As my wonderful teacher, Susan Kerr would say, *"Once you know you cannot unknow."*

Let's stay with the weight loss example. Now you know exactly what to do. Today you are going to adjust your diet and start exercising. You are flushed with excitement and optimism. Day one is a great success as you hit the gym and start your day with a healthy protein shake. This trend continues for a week, maybe even two or three. You are losing weight, feeling better and people are starting to take notice.

Then it happens, an unpleasant emotional experience. It could be anything, a call from your mother, problem at work, a cancelled date, you name it. This small disturbance is enough to trigger your emotions and send you running back to the ice cream truck. Yes, I always felt comfort with that tub of cookies and cream. The same could be said for a drink or going to the store to make a *feel-good* purchase.

You feel comfort and in strange way...**love.** It is a better feeling and you want to repeat it. This may start as a better feeling but ultimately it brings you back to the core emotion you have not addressed. I need more love and I can't seem to get it. As you drift back to your old identity the same emotional hole reappears just waiting to be filled.

In this example the feeling is tied to weight loss. You believe that once you lose weight you will receive the love you desire. This is just another example of chasing an external result to feel loved.

These exercises are based on some type of external change. You will never stop chasing if you are always focused on the external. It is the trap that will hold you hostage forever. The external world serves only one purpose for us here on earth. It reflects your internal state of emotion. I think of it as my report card. The state of my external life is just a reflection of my inner-self.

WHY YOU CAN'T SEEM TO STOP

Overcoming your DNA and millions of years of conditioning is not as easy as you might think. As humans, we are always susceptible to the trappings of the flesh. Your emotions are delicate and require much attention. The more you are connected to your feelings the easier your transition to wholeness will be.

You have been trained and conditioned to think first and feel later. You must flip this process to make the changes you seek. Now you will feel first and place your attention there. All day long I want you to keep on asking yourself-

"How do I feel?"

When I began this journey into my emotions, I was completely stuck. Feeling my emotions was a million miles from my normal state of being. Like many people, I did not grow up in an environment of open feelings and nurturing. As an Italian from New York, in this lifetime, this was not a priority. We were taught to deal with our issues and repress the problem if necessary.

As a pragmatic New Yorker I came up with a plan. I grabbed a bunch of yellow, three by five index cards. On each card, I wrote in large letters "HOW DO YOU FEEL?" I then placed these cards all over the place. In my bathroom, on my computer, in my car, on the refrigerator and any other place I knew I would see it. This started to move me into the habit of being more aware of my feelings. It brought attention to my emotions and away from the mind. It is a transformation that takes time before it becomes a habit.

You can only understand yourself and your behavior when you know what you are feeling. This will be difficult at first because you have not been conditioned to work from this position. Your level of emotional awareness will be based on your experience as a child. How emotions were dealt with at home has a major impact on your development.

Most of the people I meet describe a very dysfunctional emotional experience in childhood. Emotions were not addressed and in many cases even discouraged. This type of environment teaches a child to hide and bury emotions. Over time you will learn to reopen your feelings and go deeper. The result of this internalization of emotion can be devastating. It can lead to illness, addiction, and other destructive behavior.

Emotions are energy and your energy has to go somewhere. You may think you have successfully repressed the emotion but this is not the case. The energy you push down is still within you and it must be released. How you have learned to release it is the important issue.

What do you do when you feel stressed or uncomfortable? This will tell you how you have been conditioned to deal with your emotions.

Most of us were not really taught how to manage our feelings. This is not a skill we learned at home. The good news is you can learn it now and begin to make the changes you seek. As you become more in touch with how you feel it will be easier to understand your behavior and the results you are creating.

I want to give you a visual aid to help you see the essence of your chase.

ENERGY CYCLE

1. Energy: Everything in your life begins with energy and emotion.

2. Vibration: This emotion creates a vibration of energy.

3. Attraction: The vibration begins to attract people and situations.

4. Outcome: The cycle ends with a result.

In the energy of the chase you have a strong desire to be appreciated, accepted, noticed, recognized, and complimented. This creates a very strong feeling and starts your energy cycle. When you are chasing the feeling of love from the external world you are triggering an unresolved internal emotion. The, *I did not receive enough love feeling.*

Once you start the cycle of an external chase the wheels are in motion. You have a conscious desire to feel loved but at a deeper level you know it will not happen in the external world. This is the reason you continue to chase. You are not aware of this dynamic. Your higher-self knows the answer is within you. As your awareness and connection to your emotions grows you will no longer desire these feelings from the outside world. People will still love you and you will feel that love but you will not be chasing it.

As you would imagine this is a process and it takes time. You may be aware of it and still create a negative cycle. The difference is now you know what you created and why it happened.

THE PERILS OF THE CHASE

On June 7, 1933, a boy was born in Brooklyn, NY. He was the youngest of 12 children born to Italian immigrant parents. Times were hard as these were the days of *The Great Depression*. People struggled to survive and support themselves as the world wobbled.

His mother was already in her early forties at the time of his birth. As a result, this boy was raised by his older brothers and was tended to by his sisters. He sought the love and attention of his mother but it never came. His father was always working to support the family and offered little in the way of emotional support. As he grew up there was a huge void in his heart.

He was always trying to get attention and love from his parents but it was not forthcoming. These missing feelings became the catalyst for the chase we will examine here. The boy I speak of was my father, Joseph Nicholas Nunziata, for whom I am named.

The Nunziata family was filled with energy and life. They were natural entertainers and all fought for a position in the family spotlight. This was obviously the result of growing up in a large family with only so much attention to go around.

They were singers, dancers, comedians, and athletes. As it turned out my father was a gifted athlete, especially when it came to baseball. This was a time when baseball ruled the American sports landscape. It was truly America's game and every kid dreamed of playing for the vaunted New York Yankees. Living in New York amplified this dream to an even higher degree.

When my Dad was starting his baseball career in the early 1950's New York was the true center of the universe. There were three teams fighting for position in the biggest city in the county. The New York Yankees were the kings of the sport but the city also contained two other top teams, the Brooklyn Dodgers (now the Los Angeles Dodgers) and the New York Giants (now the San Francisco Giants).

He was a star in high school and caught the attention of some pro scouts. Two teams made offers, the Chicago Cubs, and the New York Giants. After discussing these offers with his older brothers, my Father was convinced to play for a local team and chose the Giants.

In 1951 he was sent to Oshkosh, Wisconsin to play for the Giants minor league club. He was only 18 years old at the time. My Father had never been out of Brooklyn so Oshkosh was like another planet. He struggled being separated from his family and adjusting to life as a ballplayer on the road. After just one season he left the team and retuned to Brooklyn. His dreams of becoming a professional baseball player were gone. This failure. as he saw it, haunted him for the rest of his life. As a result, the intensity of his own chase was greatly amplified.

We all experience failure and disappointment in life on some level. These setbacks can push us deeper into feelings of self-hate and unworthiness. The results are devastating, in many cases, and you can carry the emotional burden throughout your entire life. Every so-called failure, when not properly processed on an emotional level, can have an extremely negative impact on your life.

Most people were not taught the emotional skills necessary to properly deal with the many challenges we face in life. As a result, these feelings become trapped inside eroding your energy system on a daily basis. Years of chasing takes a toll on you. This may appear as a physical breakdown but it is, at the core level, an emotional collapse.

In this state of frustration and discord your mind goes into overdrive looking for the answer. How can I receive this feeling of love I so desperately need? This intense over thinking disconnects you from your spirit and true path to self-love. Now you are trapped in your mind in a frantic search for the answer.

This is the space most people live in their entire lives. A deep feeling of wanting that can never be filled. It is extremely frustrating, not to mention draining. Moving out of this cycle is the key to starting the healing process. To accomplish this, it is important to step back and stop thinking. This is easier said than done for us as overthinking humans.

MY DAD KEEPS CHASING

Following his baseball career, my Father decided to become a New York City Police Officer. Surely this would gain the attention and admiration of his mother. He would be respected and revered by everyone. They would surely love this man of honor and respect. At that time police officers were revered and respected. It was a natural choice for him.

As you would expect this did not work either. Now his brain was really humming to find the next solution. You can see how this behavior becomes so addictive. We are conditioned to chase and continue to seek an external answer. It is not our fault as this is how we are built.

My dad moved through the ranks of the police department eventually working his way up to the detective level. He was moved to the narcotics division in New York City. This was, as you would imagine, a very dirty business. It was also a departure from his activities as a uniformed police officer.

The detective's attire was called *plainclothes* (they wore ties and jackets). In addition, they were not on a set schedule like the regular policemen. This was a 24/7 type job and you had to be ready to jump at a moment's notice.

Our family life changed dramatically at that time. My father was never home and we rarely saw him for dinner. He would leave after we went to school in the morning and come home at all hours of the night, if at all. This behavior was another aspect of the chase. My father dreamed of cracking the big case. That was sure to bring him the attention and love he desired.

When you become intensely focused on the chase the rest of the world fades away. You become so obsessed with this desire that everything else loses importance. This can happen with almost anything including: your career, a certain relationship, your body, your status, and the desire to win at all costs. In this state your negative-ego completely takes over and the connection to your spirit is gone.

This may be described as egomaniacal behavior. You become possessed with someone or something and that is all you can see.

In this state, you will do whatever it takes to achieve your goal. This is often the case in the political and business arenas. How many times have we seen ruthless business people hell bent on crushing the competition or politicians manipulating situations to grab a position of power? At this point it is no longer about money or status. These people have already achieved this level of success. Now we have moved into the area of full out negative-ego. This is the chase at the highest level of intensity. The belief is that this next accomplishment will finally fill the void in your heart. When this fails, the cycle starts up again at an even higher level of intensity.

A question that often comes up is this:

How do you know when you are driving forward to accomplish something in your soul or doing it for your negative-ego?

It is the difference between creating and chasing. When you are truly creating, you are in a state of love. When you are chasing, you are in a state of fear. These are very different feelings but when you are in an obsessed state they can be difficult to discern.

Your negative-ego is extremely powerful and addictive. A feeling of power is more addictive than any drug. Like a drug, you continue to need more to achieve the same high. You can see how the addiction to power can grab you by the throat and never let go. It is intoxicating as it runs through your veins like the most powerful narcotic on earth.

So how do you know what state you are in? Once again, we return to our feelings and ask...Why am I doing this right now?

Imagine asking Michelangelo, Da Vinci or Galileo this question or asking creative business leaders, Walt Disney, or Steve Jobs.

Why are you doing this?

I saw an interview recently with singer, Sinead O'Conner. She burst on the scene with a huge hit "Nothing Compares 2 U" in 1990. The record company immediately jumped in regarding her image. They wanted here to wear short skirts and be a pop star. O'Conner said she immediately went out and cut off all her hair the next day. It was all about the music, not the image, for her.

The current state of the music industry was also discussed. Sinead talked about how the industry has evolved, all about creating marketable product and how record companies want to push new releases to capitalize on the popularity of a certain act.

Then she said something I really loved. I will paraphrase her comment.

"You shouldn't make an album unless you will die if you don't make it."

Now that is what I call creative and committed.

The question to ask is this, *am I in my heart or in my head?*

What is driving your behavior? Are you creating or controlling?

If you keep asking yourself these questions it will be easier to know where you are and why you have the desire to do something. This may seem simple but you would be amazed at how easy it is to become overtaken by fear based feelings.

We are all here to create using the most powerful force in the universe-LOVE! You are here to create based on the amazing skills and gifts you have been blessed with in this lifetime. When you live in the space of love there is no longer a reason to chase the love.

The trouble begins when we step out of this feeling. As human beings, this is challenging. You move into a lower energy when you begin to think too much. Thinking and logic are an important part of life here on earth. We must think as it is an important part of being human. The issues arise when you overthink.

How do you stop yourself from overthinking when you have been doing it your entire life?

The first step is awareness. You must be aware of something to know you are doing it. In many cases people become overwhelmed by their thoughts and react too quickly. When people overreact or act out, they are in this overwhelmed state. This state is designed to disconnect you from your true feelings. I have seen people yell, scream and cry in this condition. It looks like they are being emotional but they are trapped in a negative mental cycle.

When you realize your mind is beginning to race it is time to put on the brakes. As I said, this can happen quickly and take over in a hurry. Your awareness and recognition will be your first line of defense. The minute you see this happening stop what you are doing. This is the time to disengage your mind and connect with your emotions. Being in nature is a great way to ground your energy and I recommend a nice quiet walk. The key is breaking the energy. You may just go get a cup of coffee, read the newspaper, or play some music. Do whatever works for you. Music is great because it carries vibration that will adjust your energy frequency. There are no hard and fast rules here.

Now you have stopped the cycle from gaining momentum. You have broken the desire to chase and grounded your energy.

Now you can go back to your activity in a different space. Meditation is also a great tool that I will discuss later.

The desire to chase runs deep so do not get a false sense of security. You must remain vigilant and aware of your feelings. Every time the feeling comes up and your mind starts racing use your tools to stop it. Go back to your core questions.

» Why am I doing this?

» Am I in my heart or in my head?

» Am I creating or controlling?

These three questions will help you create a much higher awareness and a deeper connection to your true desires. When you are completely honest with your feelings you are in the highest state of energy possible.

There will be times when you will not like what you are feeling. It is okay; the key is being honest with how you really feel.

THE BIG SCORE

3

MY FATHER BECAME entrenched in his detective identity. It was a life filled with distortion and blurred reality. His job was busting drug dealers but to do so he had to befriend criminals and underworld figures. This was an exciting life on many levels. There was plenty of chasing, socializing and excitement. It was the ultimate cat and mouse game.

He worked with a special unit of detectives in the narcotics squad called SIU (Special Investigative Unit). Two of these detectives would become famous for breaking the "French Connection" case. The story spawned a book in 1969 and then a movie two years later. This case vaulted the detectives who broke it, Sonny Grosso and Eddie Egan, to star status at the time.

This development sent my Father into overdrive. Now he imagined himself breaking an even bigger case and becoming even more famous than his colleagues. Once again, we find ourselves in chasing mode. It is now time to go back to our three questions and see where this situation falls.

1. Why am I doing this? To become famous and receive the love I desire.

2. Am I in my heart or in my head? My head, this is all external and ego driven.

3.   Am I creating or controlling? I am trying to control the outcome to create personal glory.

My Father did not have these questions or the awareness to truly understand his motivation at the time. He continued his quest obsessing over the big case he would break. He never realized he was the little boy in Brooklyn desperately seeking his mother's attention.

His external transformation, not unlike that of Darth Vader, was now complete. If you are a Star Wars fan you know the story of Anakin Skywalker. He begins as a gifted child with a desire to help the universe but is ultimately overtaken by the allure of the *Dark Side*. Eventually he aligns with an evil dark lord, and the rest is history.

My father was not a bad person but he moved into a dark place. He was overtaken by the emotion of the chase. My Father was driven by the hole in his heart and could never figure out how to fill it. These are common themes for all of us here in the physical world. The ability to achieve balance is a never-ending challenge for all of us. Remaining perfectly balanced is virtually impossible all we can do is remain aware and continue to adjust.

As his obsession grew he was becoming further removed from his family and anyone else who was not part of his chase. His immersion into this world was so deep he was unable to see anything else. This is the proverbial carrot at the end of the stick. You are constantly grasping but never actually getting it.

It is very easy to become caught up in this life here on earth. In spiritual terms, it is classified as living a very third dimensional life. We are spiritual beings living a physical experience. Most humans see themselves as physical beings living a physical experience.

The term **third dimension** refers to your level of awareness and consciousness. As we become more aware we realize that there are higher levels of energy and consciousness to attain. In higher states of energy, the trappings of the physical world are not important. Your desire to be your best-self at the highest spiritual level is much more exciting.

When you live a third dimensional life you are attached to the physical world.

This is what is important to people on a third dimensional level:

» Your identity
» Your possessions
» Your position in society
» Your perceived level of power
» Your career
» Your status

As you read this list you can see how most people here on earth are trapped in this reality. They are always pushing for the next thing. It may be a physical possession like a bigger home or expensive car. When people achieve financial success these physical objects are not enough to fill the void. They move past the objects and seek more power or higher status. At this point you are trapped in a cycle that will never end. There will always be someone with more be it material possessions or power.

"The Big Score" is "The Big Trap."

Most of our population continues to spin like tops on this never-ending cycle of acquisition. A top spins and spins until it runs out of energy and eventually just falls over to the side. This is how most people go through life here on earth as they live a third dimensional existence.

It is an exhausting journey with no pot of gold at the end of the rainbow. Most are ultimately unfulfilled and emotionally spent before their departure from the physical world. This is the ultimate ending for those who go through life in search of the love they never received in the form of external possessions. The majority will never know why they ended up in such a state as their level of awareness here on earth was not high enough to know better. This is not meant to be a judgment. It is a statement based on where we are in our human development. The good news is we are all moving to higher levels of awareness.

OUT OF THE CAVES

Our ancestors lived in very different state of energy and awareness based on circumstance. Their number one concern was finding enough to eat and looking for a safe place to sleep. This, of course, required all their energy and attention. There was a not a lot of energy left over for self-contemplation or inner thinking.

Today we do not face the same issues. Food and safe places to sleep are readily available without much concern for many people. This gives us the ability to use our new-found time and energy for a higher purpose. We can choose to contemplate life at a much deeper level.

Notice I said, *we can choose*. We now have the time and energy to go deeper, but we must also have the desire to do so. This takes commitment and courage on our part. Most people would prefer to look the other way. It is much easier to take a vacation or remodel your kitchen than to look at your true self.

Our society has become very adept at creating distractions. We have amusement parks, casinos, beach resorts and a host of other options to distract us from ourselves. I am not suggesting you should not enjoy all the physical world has to offer. The key is, knowing the difference between creating a distraction and enjoying the physical world.

I worked with a client who was constantly remodeling her home. The minute one area was completed she moved on the next. When she finally remodeled the entire house, she moved on to the furniture. This was not about joy, it was about distraction.

Creating a distraction is a great way to avoid your feelings and issues. It is time to examine yourself in this area. Do you continue to create distractions to avoid dealing with your issues? There are many ways to create these distractions. Home remodeling is just one of your choices.

Another tactic is creating drama and upset. When things are moving smoothly it affords you the time for self-reflection. To avoid this situation, you create drama to fill in the void. Creating drama is a sabotage technique that holds you in a negative cycle and moves you away from your true issues. When you become caught up in the drama there is no time to address your own issues. You see how smart we are when it comes to avoiding our true feelings.

Making yourself very busy is another great distraction you can easily justify. It is such an easy sell to your family and friends. You get to feel important and people say things like, "how does she get it all done?" Wow! Doesn't that feel great? This is another way to fill your ego's desire and avoid your deeper issues.

Your negative ego wants to hold you in the cycle of chasing. This is accomplished by keeping you focused on the physical world. The more you identify with your possessions and title the further you are from your true self. If you see yourself as the president of the company with the big house and fancy car you are deeply entrenched in your negative ego identity. How important is this identity? The answer to this question will tell you exactly where you are in relation to your higher-self.

The more importance you give to the external world the further you are from enlightenment and freedom. This is a very interesting part of the journey as you need an identity to have a physical experience here on earth. Understand and accept this truth but know you do not have to be overtaken by this identity. It is a tool you are using to have this wonderful experience in the physical world.

Imagine yourself with no identity. It feels strange to have no title, possessions, accomplishments, or other worldly attachments. How would you feel if you were free? If you were not concerned about what others thought or how you were perceived? If material success was a non-issue and the way you looked physically was of no consequence. How would you feel in this circumstance?

As you move into the light your priorities are shifted. Your attachment to the trappings of the physical world begin to dissolve. Things that were so important to you before like the big house, new car or job title no longer hold you hostage. You have been held hostage by these ideas and concepts your entire life. Now you will become free of such beliefs and desires. I must say this is a very liberating experience. Once again, this does not mean you cannot enjoy all the wonderful things we have here on earth. The difference is, now you are enjoying it without the emotional attachment. The importance has been removed making for a much more joyful experience.

In higher energy, you realize there is no need for the big score because every day you are here is the big score. Every emotion and experience is a fabulous part of your journey. The happy and the sad, the success and the failure, the excitement and the pain are all part of your whole experience.

There is no need to chase because it serves no purpose. I know what you are thinking, but what am I supposed to do now? Should I just sit around waiting to feel something and experience the emotion?

Not exactly! It is time to see how our nature makes us great and creates much of our pain and suffering. We are all coins with two sides. Learning to balance these two sides is one of the keys to creating your life at the highest level.

HUMANS, WE ARE SUCH MALCONTENTS

4

O
NE OF MY CLOSEST FRIENDS growing up was Joe Brennan. We continue to be best of friends to this day. Joe grew up in a traditional big Irish family of 10 kids. His father Bill was an amazing guy. He was always very interested in personal development and loved the fact that we had jumped into this work at an early age. There were many evenings when we sat in Joe's living room talking to his dad. He reminded me of the great UCLA basketball coach John Wooden. He looked like Wooden and also had the wisdom and compassion.

He would always come out with interesting observations and words of wisdom. One of my favorites was...*your strength is your weakness*. The first time I heard this statement I was confused. How could my strength be my weakness? What could be bad about being good at something? As time passed I gained a much greater understanding of this principle and now see how it applies to all people.

Once again it requires us to step out of our normal way of thinking and seeing the world. The more you step out of your mind and expand the more powerful you will become. Question

---

everything you know and be open to a different view. This philosophy allows you to see things most people never see.

What makes human beings great is also what creates so much pain and suffering. Humans are seekers which does have a natural element of chasing built into it. When you are always seeking something better it is easy to slip right into overdrive and start a fabulous chase.

As seekers, we are also inventors. We are always looking for a way to do something more efficiently, faster, and easier. Without this quality, we would all still be living in caves. It is this desire to create and improve that makes us so amazing. This would be considered a great strength of the species. I know what you are thinking, why does this desire to always improve make us malcontents?

This is where the weakness comes into play. The desire to always improve moves us into a state of unrest and dissatisfaction. I have this job but I should have a better one. I like this house but I want a bigger one. This car is nice but I really like that one.

I am sure you can see how this tendency can create a real problem. How do we embrace the fact that we are malcontents and rejoice in all we have accomplished at the same time? This is a riddle for our species to solve if we are to live enlightened lives.

Our Malcontent DNA is the perfect fuel for the chase we find ourselves engaged in here on earth. We constantly want to make our lives better. In most cultures this trait is revered and encouraged. It is like throwing gasoline on the fire.

People will describe you as driven, motivated, persistent, and unstoppable. These are the wonderful traits we find in successful people. Why would you want to give this up when you know it is critical to your success? You do not have to give it up but you do want to understand all aspects of it.

You must be aware of what is driving your behavior. By aware I mean understanding the feeling that is at the heart of your desire. Your mind will attempt to trick you and create a justification for your behavior. It is important to move past your mind and go into how you truly feel.

I remember speaking to a group of insurance agents in New York City. In an exercise, I had all the agents write down one thing they really wanted to acquire in the next year.

One of the agent's, a sharp looking guy in his mid-thirties with perfect hair and an impeccable blue suit shared his answer with the group. I want a Mercedes C-Class, silver with black interior. He went on to describe all the features plus the bells and whistles he desired.

"That's great," I replied, "You know exactly what you want and have a very clear picture." A big smile filled his face. He looked like the cat that ate the canary.

Then I asked him my favorite questions:

» Why do you want that car?

» Why is that so important to you?

His smile quickly faded away and I could see the gears in his head churning to come up with the right answer. The problem, for this slick insurance agent, was there is no right answer.

After a few minutes he said, "It will make me feel like I have reached the success I deserve for all my hard work." A lesser grin returned to his face after these words were delivered.

Then I posed another question, "Why do you need a car to feel successful?"

Once again, he was stumped. He mumbled and stumbled to justify his answer for a few minutes. I asked to him to look inside himself for the truth.

"Why do you really want that car?" I queried.

He hesitated and finally cried out, "I want to drive through my old neighborhood so everyone can see how successful I have become."

His shoulders slumped as if all the tension in his body had been removed. It was an amazing sight to see as he physically transformed into a different person in front of everyone in the room. I went on to describe how his desire was 100% ego driven. When we are reacting to the desires of the negative-ego we are destined to chase forever. This creates a never-ending cycle of dissatisfaction. You are forever chasing the carrot at the end of the stick.

I know what you are thinking...Joe does this mean I can never have a "Mercedes"?

This has nothing to do with the Mercedes. It is all about the feeling driving you to acquire the Mercedes. The ego wants it for validation, your higher-self wants the joy of the experience. Why do you want it?

It is very simple to see but difficult for us to balance as human beings. Any time you have an external desire you are being driven by your negative-ego. You want to accomplish or attain something to prove yourself. In most cases, you want others to see what you have so they will know you have value. Most humans work from this position most of their lives. As you would imagine this is a wild rollercoaster ride with a crash and burn ending.

An internal feeling is tied to your soul. The feeling generated in this space is love and joy. You desire something because it will bring you a feeling of love and joy. Creative people who are connected to their spirit never talk about money or possessions. They talk about creation, joy and making the world a better place. That is a true internal feeling and it is your key to happiness.

I know, I know, what about the Mercedes.

If driving a Mercedes brings you great joy, then having it is a wonderful experience. You are not concerned with showing off to others and creating status. It is tied to the joy you have when driving the car. The same rules apply to all material possessions. We are living in a material world and having certain physical possessions is part of the game. The important thing is not losing your soul in a mad search for power and status.

HOW DO YOU REALLY FEEL?

I have always found the best way to uncover my true feelings is through meditation. If you are not a meditator don't be alarmed. Just get quiet to uncover your feelings. The most important thing is being honest about how you really feel.

Your truth is tied to how you feel and this is the key to uncovering your blocks and hidden desires.

We live in a society filled with noise and distraction. Moving into a quiet space has become more challenging than ever. Make it a priority to carve out quiet time each day. It does not have to be long just consistent. This will have a very positive impact on your life and well-being.

Meditation is nothing more than disconnecting from your mind. This seemingly simple action is not as easy as it sounds.

Find a quiet spot and select a time when you will not be interrupted. Do not lie down because your brain will move into sleep mode. You should be sitting up preferably on the floor. You can lean against the wall, bed, a chair, whatever is most comfortable. If you cannot sit on the floor use a comfortable chair but be sure to sit up.

Begin with a few deep inhales and exhales on a count of three. Inhale on a three count and then exhale on a three count. You do not have to say it just keep a silent count. In a few minutes you will become more relaxed and disconnected from your mind.

Focus on something you want to create in your life. It could be anything, a new car, start a business, writing a book, whatever you truly desire. Do not allow your mind to jump in with logic. Something like, you are too old to start a business now. If these thoughts pop into your head gently let them go. Then refocus on your desire and hold that energy.

What is the feeling that comes up when you see yourself creating what you desire? You may have a few surface feelings like excitement or exhilaration at first. Then you begin to go deeper into the true feeling. What are you really feeling? Is there an external attachment like, this will show them how good I am or is there a feeling of bliss? It is important to be honest to uncover your true feelings. Just like the insurance agent with the Mercedes.

When your desire is tied to feelings of love and joy you are on the right track. Just *Follow Your Bliss* as Joseph Campbell proclaimed in one of his many inspirational writings. At this point you are connected to yourself and the power of the universe at the highest level. Now you will need the courage to follow through regardless of the obstacles you will face.

Many people believe that once you make this connection the path is cleared in an instant. I am here to tell you this is only the beginning of your journey. All accomplishments require work and dedication before they come to fruition. This does not mean you must suffer. You may struggle and deal with obstacles but this is all part of the growing process. The good news is you are on the right path.

What happens when you are honest with your feelings and realize your desire is tied to an external outcome? Be honest about this revelation to truly move yourself to a higher level of consciousness. Your mind will jump in again and try to trick you. This is accomplished through justification and rationalization. Keep going back to your feeling and connect to your joy.

THE ROMAN EMPIRE WAS BUILT ON A HUGE EGO TRIP

I will never forget a guy I met named Frank in the dry-cleaning business when I was selling advertising. He had a successful store, but wanted to expand like most business owners and entrepreneurs. The desire to expand is natural and healthy for all of us. Frank was a very driven guy. He was a perfectionist and was extremely demanding of his employees, family, and friends. He was a true type "A" personality who wanted to win at all costs. Once again, we have some of the traits we admire in successful people.

His desire was to open more stores in the region and then move into other markets. I asked Frank why he wanted to do this and he replied, "*I want to crush the competition and own the region."* As you noticed this is not a desire based on love and joy. The word *crush* gave it away for me. In this situation, negative energy drove Frank. He may become successful like many others from a business perspective. The question is; will he be successful from a soul perspective?

What happens to Frank after he crushes the competition and dominates the market? If you follow history the answer is simple, he moves on to the next market. Kind of like the Roman Empire. This energy traps Frank (as it did the Romans) in a never-ending cycle of chasing the next market or region to conquer. Eventually this energy collapses on itself. The end of the story is already written based on the starting point. When you start with negative energy, you end in despair.

This is a great lesson for us as Roman society mirrors our current state of affairs. A small percentage of people had all the money and power. Many people were poor or slaves. The Romans had an overwhelming desire to conquer and control more people. Does this sound familiar?

The Roman Empire was not conquered. It collapsed from within and was then overrun by barbarians. This society lacked balance and love. The universe seeks balance and it will always balance the scales. It may take some time but it will always rebalance itself.

This is a lesson for all of us as we chase our desires here on earth. Be careful and be aware of your motivation. Your mind will constantly attempt to trick you like the snake in the Garden of Eden. Be true to your feelings and you will always move with a higher purpose.

I AM IN TOO DEEP NOW

5

ONE EVENING MY FATHER received a phone call at home from a friend. He was a Sergeant on the force my dad had known for many years. This was the call my father had been waiting for his entire life. The Sergeant had a tip on a big drug dealer named Carlo coming in from Italy. He was tied up with another case and could not follow up on this hot lead. My father, in full chasing mode, jumped all over this opportunity.

The Sergeant called my dad because he respected him as a detective. What he did not know was the lead was a set-up. There was a lot of corruption in the New York City Police Department at that time and the higher ups were setting traps for police officers. They were trying to flush out the corrupt cops and clean up the department.

This call was targeting the Sergeant who they thought was corrupt. He was supposed to follow-up this lead regarding the Italian drug dealer. Carlo, the drug dealer, was going to offer a bribe and then trap the Sergeant. When my father received the call, he was thrown into the middle of this web with no knowledge of the situation.

I learned about this story years later and no idea this was happening at the time. There were many nights when I sat around contemplating what might have been. What if my father was out and the Sergeant then passed the lead on to someone else? This was the 1970's there were no cell phones or pagers.

The imagined outcomes played on my mind. I remember thinking; this one phone call completely changed my life. It was something that took only a few seconds and it changed everything. It was an innocent phone call from a guy who wanted to help a friend. There was no bad intention or malice involved.

I drove myself crazy with possible scenarios and different outcomes. It took many years for me to truly accept what happened and move to a peaceful place with this situation. Acceptance has become an important part of my work and life.

My father recruited some of his detective friends and they went to arrest the Italian drug dealer at a hotel in lower Manhattan. They busted into the room, cuffed him, and brought him to a holding facility in downtown Manhattan. Carlo knew immediately that something had gone wrong. This was an elaborate set-up and it was not going as scripted. Had the Sergeant made the arrest he would have taken Carlo to a different facility. Carlo called the higher-ups in the New York Police Department to explain what had happened.

These department heads proceeded to call my father. They told him to let Carlo go as he was to be taken to a different department for processing. This was the opportunity my father had to let it go. The universe gave him a choice and he made his based on his ego and desire to be important. Had he agreed, that would have been the end of the story.

My dad was now in overdrive and there was no way he was going to let this guy go. This was the big score he had been waiting for his entire life.

Once again, I had a case of the-what if's.

As I learned more about spiritual work and destiny I often wondered if this was his divine plan. Was he destined to go down this road of self-destruction and heartache? The universe gave him the opportunity to take a different path but he chose to stay on this one. Was this predestined or could he have made another choice? As human's we have the power of free will. We face a series of decisions every day. Many are quite mundane, what to eat, what to wear, where to go meet your friend for coffee. Others are much more impactful. Who you marry, what you do for living, where you live and the path you follow carry much more weight.

What would have happened if my father walked away and let Carlo go? Based on his energy and karma I fear he would have found himself in a similar situation again soon. He was in chase mode and his fate was already sealed. In this lifetime, he was born to chase.

Once you are in chase mode it is very difficult to get off the wheel. You are now entrenched in an endless cycle of needing more. This is the place many people in modern society find themselves today. They came out of school chasing the life they believe they were supposed to have to be happy. You have the house, the spouse, two cars and 2.5 kids on board. You arrived here by taking a job you didn't really want, received a few promotions, starting making more money and reached an income level to maintain a lifestyle you really don't need. Ouch, now what?

You are in too deep now. How can you walk up to your significant other and proclaim your desire to become a sculptor? This is the result of chasing stuff and we have all been there. Now you feel trapped in a situation of your own creation. This is an extremely frustrating situation and it can lead people down some dark paths.

The feeling of frustration creates an internal combustion. You have a desire to make a change but feel you are unable to do so. There is a part of you that feels responsible. This creates an internal battle of desire vs. frustration.

The longer you hold this energy the worse it gets. It builds up inside you and begins to create issues. If you do not deal with it in a constructive way it will create negative situations in your life. Holding frustration and deep sadness creates intense inner pain. It is important to process this emotion in a positive way to heal the pain.

There are three roads you can take when dealing with emotions. Most people are not aware of the healing option and they continue to create pain and suffering.

These are your options:

1. You internalize and create illness, physical issues, and depression

2. You act out using the external world to vent your frustration (alcohol, drugs, eating, shopping, work, violence, drama, etc.)

3. You release the energy and cleanse your system of it (this is the high road)

Most people are not aware of Option 3 so they choose "Options 1 or 2" by default. It is not your fault, you are not aware there is another option.

Your emotions are energy and your energy is always moving. When you repress your feelings, they sit in your body and begin to manifest in physical issues, illnesses, or other destructive events.

OPTION 1: INTERNALIZING

In this case, you have been trained to stuff your feelings down. You were taught that expressing your emotions is a bad thing. Look back to your childhood and think about how emotions were handled in your family. Most people have no idea how to deal with emotions in a constructive manner. Your parents followed the model of their parents regarding the management of emotions. This creates a chain of dysfunction which continues from one generation to the next. The cycle continues until someone decides to step out and break it.

If you are an emotional stuffer it is important to be aware of this behavior. The energy you are holding will create destructive situations in your life. As you continue to push the emotions down the energy is becoming stronger. Eventually this backed up energy starts creating problems. Depression and physical illness are common for those who repress their emotions and energy.

OPTION 2: ACTING OUT

This is the opposite of internalizing. In this case, instead of holding the emotions in, you want to get rid of them as soon as possible. Acting out is how a person manipulates energy to avoid dealing with their feelings by pushing the energy and emotion away from themselves.

We all have *go-to* stress reducing activities. In moderation, these activities can be healthy and beneficial. You may go to the gym, have a drink, or eat some comfort food. Eventually you must deal with the emotions that are coming up.

One of my favorite things to do is go to the movies. When I am feeling a little worn out or drained, I go to a matinee. This gives me a few hours to disconnect and recharge my batteries. Other good options are connecting with nature, the beach, a walk in the park, etc, you can also exercise or get a massage. These are all positive things we can do to reduce stress.

Acting out is different because it is used to pull you out of your feelings. What do you do when you get upset? Drinking, yelling, shopping, eating, working, cleaning; the list is endless. The difference here is the intensity of the action. There is a heightened feeling and a strong desire to rid yourself of the emotion as fast as you can.

This will also be based on an emotional trigger, like the boss who made a negative comment. You have all this energy and you don't know what to do with it. It is like trying to put a tornado in a box. You can't control it so the next best option is to get it away from you.

You have an unresolved emotion that you do not want to address. Instead of dealing with the feeling you have been conditioned to act out. Look at your parents and you will see where you learned this behavior.

The same rules apply here. Instead of going into your routine, stop and ask yourself: How do I feel?

It is the exact same thing as internalizing from an energy perspective because you are still holding the energy. In both cases, you are not dealing with the emotion that is coming up. As you would imagine learning to address your feelings takes practice and commitment.

Remember your new favorite question: How do I feel?

OPTION 3: CLEARING YOUR ENERGY

As an enlightened person, you are unhappy with the situation and begin to seek better options. You become an adventurer in search of a better way to live your life.

As the Christopher Columbus of your family you are breaking the rules and challenging old beliefs and systems. The people who are deeply entrenched in the family drama are not interested in the exploits of Christopher Columbus. They like the drama and dysfunction of this world. They have no desire to change any aspect of the situation. That is fine for them and you must allow them to stay in that space if they so choose. I have learned over the years that you must desire a change and be willing to work to create it. Trying to force others to change is a painful road to go down.

This is the high-level option. Your awareness and desire to release this negative energy in a positive way will make all the difference in your life. Instead of repressing or acting out you will deal with these feelings and emotions head on.

The key is addressing your issues as quickly as possible, releasing the energy, and moving forward. It is a process that takes time to master, but you will see benefits right away.

The best medicine is to be aware of how you feel and then allow yourself to feel the emotions that are coming up. I say "allow" because to this point you have not been allowing yourself to feel based on what you learned as a child. You may have been conditioned to believe feelings are bad so you repress them, act out or ignore them completely. Now you will shift the way you see and deal with your emotions.

The next time something upsets you take a moment and ask yourself this question: "How do I feel?" This is going to become your new mantra. Time to identify the feeling.

Let's say your boss made a comment about you. Ordinarily, you would just let it go by and make an excuse for your boss. Now I want you to stop and ask yourself, "How do I feel?" Perhaps he said something about your organizational skills. Initially you feel upset by the comment. How could he say that, after all I do for him? Being upset is your surface feeling but you must go deeper to get to the root of the issue. As you move beyond the surface feeling there is a deeper emotion to explore.

This is where the work requires extra effort. To clear the negative energy, you must identify the real emotion and feel it.

As you move past the initial feeling of being upset you go deeper to identify the true emotion. I would like to take a moment to clarify feelings and emotions as I am using them in this example. These are interchangeable terms on some level but in energy clearing work they take on a distinct meaning.

Surface Feelings: These are the initial feelings that come up in an uncomfortable or stressful situation. Such feelings bring unresolved, emotional inner conflicts to your attention. They are surges of energy connected to deeper emotional issues.

Surface Feelings Include:

» Anger

» Upset

» Disgusted

- » Annoyed
- » Frustrated
- » Worried
- » Anxious

In the boss example, you may have been upset with by the comment. That was the surface feeling that got your attention.

True Emotions: The emotions you are experiencing at a deeper level. Your emotions are tied to your soul, karma, DNA, and journey.

When you experience a surface feeling the next step is to stop and ask yourself, what am I really feeling? As you sit with this for a while, the true emotion will surface. In this case the true emotion was that of being unappreciated.

That is the emotion you are holding onto since childhood. You break the negative energy by allowing yourself to feel that emotion thus releasing the energy from your body.

True Emotions Include:

- » Unloved
- » Unworthy
- » Unappreciated
- » Abandoned
- » Loneliness
- » Fear
- » Unsafe
- » Incompetent
- » Responsibility
- » Disappointment

Most people stop at upset (the surface feeling) and never go deeper as they were not taught to do so. This is the difference between feelings and emotions. Feelings get your attention; the true emotion holds the energy and creates situations in your life.

ENERGY RELEASING PROCESS

Step 1-Be Aware of Your Feelings

Step 2-Bring Up a Recent Issue (Like the example of the boss)

Step 3-Identify What You Were Feeling

    -Surface Feeling the True Emotion

Step 4-Link the Emotion to Your Past. What Does this
    remind you of from Your Childhood?

Step 5-Allow Yourself to Feel the Emotion

MEDITATION PROCESS

The best way I have found to clear the energy is through a meditative process. Find a quiet place in your home and make sure you will not be disturbed. Visualize the event that brought up the emotion. See the event as if you were watching a movie. As you go deeper move into what you were feeling as the event took place. How did you feel when the boss made that comment?

In this example, the true emotion identified was not feeling appreciated.

Next question: Who made you feel unappreciated as a child?

The answer will be mom or dad or both.

Bringing up these feelings may trigger an old memory; an incident that occurred in childhood when you felt the exact same feeling. This is the core of the energy you have been holding on to all these years, because you are holding this unresolved feeling you continue to recreate the same scenario with different people. Your energy is attracting the same situation over and over again.

In your meditative state go back to your childhood and ask yourself, who made me feel this way when I was a child? This will bring you to one of your parents. It may trigger a specific event from your childhood. This will bring up a surge of emotion.

As you move through this process it will bring up feelings about your parents. You may be angry at the way they treated you and even hate them for it. Your core emotions will be anchored to your parents. The key here is allowing yourself to feel the emotion without judgment.

Your emotions are not good or bad. They exist as part of your life. Do not judge yourself or your parents, by thinking you did something wrong. Judgment will move you into a mental state and take you out of your emotions.

It may take you some time to let go of the judgment. That is a natural part of the process. In time, you will release your judgments and let the energy go.

The energy is released when you allow yourself to feel it on an emotional level. Sit quietly and replay the episode in your mind. As you do this, let the emotion flow through you. Do not judge the emotion as good or bad, right, or wrong. Just feel it as deeply as possible. Continue to repeat this process as more emotions come into your awareness.

Your awareness of this cycle is the beginning of the healing process. When you allow yourself to feel the pain you have been repressing, the energy is released. Once the energy is released you will stop creating situations in which you feel unappreciated.

Be aware that these feelings are layered and take time to be completely removed. You may create a similar situation to a lesser degree. This will happen until you have fully addressed all aspects of the emotion you are clearing.

You will know the energy is gone when you do not feel the emotional charge attached to the specific emotion. At this point you are no longer carrying the negative energy. You have now removed this emotional trigger at the core level.

As the energy is released you are changing your vibration. In your new vibration of energy, you will no longer desire the negative feeling you released. In this example, not being appreciated. Now you will begin to attract people who appreciate you.

Please don't overcomplicate this process. Remember, it is not a mental game, it is an emotional game.

In this example the boss made the comment that triggered a feeling in you. It is not necessary to address him, as he is simply the messenger. You created that situation to bring the feeling into your consciousness. If anything, you should thank him for his help.

Remember, the energy is released when you allow yourself to feel the pain and emotion you have been repressing.

ALIGNING YOUR BODY'S ENERGY

Every time you feel emotions at the core level and release the energy, your physical body goes through a transition. You have let go of negative energy you have been carrying for many years and your body needs some time to adjust.

The cells in your body are always recoding. When you release negative energy, you are recoding your cells with new energy. You are changing your core DNA as you transform.

You may also experience physical symptoms such as: runny nose, cold, body aches, fatigue, flu-like symptoms, headaches. This is how your physical body removes dense energy.

I want you to be aware of how you will feel as you move through this process of clearing your energy field.

RESTORATION PROCESS

Now that you have removed negative energy which is a huge accomplishment. It is time to restore yourself with positive energy. You want to replace the negative energy you just let go of with strong positive feelings.

Once again, meditation is a great way to elevate your energy.

Sit quietly and see a brilliant white light over your head. Bring the white light down through the crown of your skull. Imagine this light entering at the top of your head and slowly bring it down through each energy (Chakra Point) of your body.

Move the light slowly down to your forehead, nose and mouth, throat, heart, solar plexus, pelvic area, down to the base of your spine. Expand the light until your entire body is glowing in this brilliant white light. Feel the love of the universe pulsing through you and know you are a perfect expression of love.

Love yourself and know you are perfect. Accept everything about yourself and know that you are pure love. Hold this energy and allow yourself to feel this amazing power flow through you.

You can use this meditation after a release or to increase your energy flow at any time. The more you feel love and power, the better your life will become.

THERE IS ALWAYS HOPE

There are times in life when you feel like all hope is lost. Every human being on the planet has felt this feeling at one time or another. We are resilient creatures, but we all have a breaking point.

I love this Hemingway quote, *"The world breaks everyone, and afterward, some are strong at the broken places."*

Being in too deep creates a feeling of despair, you see your situation as overwhelming or unresolvable. This can occur in your relationships, finances, career, or health. After years of struggle and heartache, you feel compelled to just throw in the towel.

This feeling is the result of losing control. You feel the situation has gotten away from you and you cannot see a way to fix it.

Your desire to manipulate or control a situation is based on fear. These feelings are tied to your primal desire to feel safe. If you can get control of all aspects of your life you will be safe. As you know, this is not possible but it does not stop you from trying to make it so.

You are trying to create an outcome based on your fears. When you fail to create this outcome, you become frustrated and eventually lose hope. I have heard so many people say things like, *"I've done everything to make this work and it just isn't happening."* Frustrating indeed!

This is also tied to chasing a situation you want to create. Why do you have to chase it? What would happen if you did not chase it?

You can work towards something without feeling frantic and stressed. This is how you shift away from chasing. As chasers, we create a lot undue stress by installing expectations and deadlines. Some people may see these as goals.

There is nothing wrong with setting goals. Having a goal, a target, a dream is what life is all about for us humans. There is a desire to make a change or accomplish something.

Before you begin your quest, it is important to ask yourself a question: Why do I want to do this now? This is the same question I presented to you earlier in the chasing example. As you can see these things are tied together.

You must feel something powerful to move forward. Do you really want to do it or do you feel you should do it? Is this your desire or the desire of others?

Who are you trying to make happy? This is another great question to ask before taking the first step. Please be honest with your answers to truly move forward in a positive way.

Let's say you have decided you want to write a book: this is something you have always dreamed of doing. You feel it all the way down to your toenails. The next thing that tends to happen is the thinking process. Because you have never written a book you do not know how to accomplish this task. Over-thinking is where your dreams go to die. You start thinking about how to do it. Your palms begin to sweat and fear of failure creeps into your head. Instead of starting and becoming disappointed you will stop this insanity right now.

Wait a minute, this time you are determined and things will be different. You decide to move forward even though you have no idea how to make this happen. Don't worry about how to make it happen. The most important thing is to just begin the process. This step shifts your energy and begins your transformation.

The next thing many people do is attach expectations and deadlines. Now the game has been changed. This attachment has moved you from an organic creative process to a restricted mental process. It is important to stay in your creative flow as you move forward. You can set goals and expectations as long as you do not become too attached to them.

Life is always creating unexpected twists and turns for us. Being completely attached to your goals, expectations and deadlines will create unnecessary pain and suffering. You do not really need any of these things, but as humans we like to have some structure.

When you are dealing with creation there are no fixed rules or exact processes to follow. You are inspired to create and that is it. Your brain wants to jump in and say, "I will complete my book within 12-months." All changes are organic and they do not conform to a specific time line. If you do not complete the book in 12 months you are not a failure, unless you see yourself as such.

I was watching a show about Academy Award winning director, Martin Scorsese. He was discussing his creative process and many of the great films he has made. At one point, he opened an old spiral notebook. It looked as if he had been carrying this thing around since high school.

He was discussing the film *Gangs of New York*. Scorsese opened the old spiral notebook to a specific drawing. It was a drawing of a scene he had envisioned for the film some 20 years earlier. He discussed the scene and the ideas he had been contemplating for the film over the years. His vision became a reality more than 20 years after he originally started writing his notes.

We may have our calendar, but the universe has another version. The universe's plan is designed for your highest and greatest good. You may believe you are in too deep and have many reasons why you cannot create the life you desire at this time. When this happens, take a moment, and know the universe has the perfect plan for you.

I AM SO CLOSE I CAN TASTE IT

6

YOUR NEGATIVE EGO IS A dangerous and tricky son of a gun. It loves to entice you by dangling just enough of what you think you want right in front of you. When you are emotionally invested in these desires, it is very difficult to take a step back.

We return to my father's chase as he was now right in the middle of this process. He had his big case and was blinded to any other option or possibility. His refusal to let go of Carlo set off another chain reaction. He upset the higher-ups in the police department who had spent months setting up this sting operation. They decided to turn the tables on him and continue the sting with a new target...him.

When you are caught up in the chase you cannot see anything else. You are in a tunnel with a narrow view of what is happening in front of you. All other aspects of your life lose importance and value. You are now fully committed to the chase. In poker terms, you are all in.

Once you push all your chips to the center of the table, there is no turning back. Even if you want to back out, you just can't seem to do it. This is a tricky part of the human experience.

You have a desire you have been working towards for a long time. Staying focused and moving forward is a critical piece of the puzzle. Believing in yourself and not quitting is a trait successful people share. How do you know when to step back and when to push forward? Again, we go back to your feelings.

» Why are you doing it?

» Why do you want to keep on pushing forward?

» What are you feeling?

These are important questions to answer because they tell you where you are on the inside. My father was chasing the respect and attention he never received from his mother. This was not a pure intention coming from his soul, it was a feeling based on unresolved emotions, ego, and the desire to feel loved. Unresolved emotions drive many people their entire lives.

We are all seeking approval on some level and have been conditioned to believe that an external accomplishment or possession will fill the void. This is the core of the chase, and it does not end well for most of us.

THE TABLES TURN

My father believed he had gotten exactly what he wanted when they turned Carlo back over to him. Now he could make his big case and receive all the attention and respect he so desperately wanted. What he did not know was, there was no big case or glory waiting for him. He was now in the middle of a sting designed to trap him.

The stage was set and the outcome was already determined. The only question, how would this all play out? It would have been a great piece of theatre had it not been a real-life story.

Carlo knew what my father wanted and he relayed this message to his superiors. "This guy is not about money, he wants glory," Carlo reported. Equipped with this information Carlo was now able to create the perfect manipulation. He knew exactly how to suck my dad in, keep him interested and set-up the final act of this elaborate play.

He continued to tell my father about some huge drug shipments that were being planned. My dad was salivating and Carlo knew exactly what to feed him. This dance went on for some time until my father started to lose his patience. He began pressing Carlo and threatening him with deportation. The final chapter of the story was now ready to unfold.

They set a meeting at a restaurant in New York City. It would be my father, his partner, Louis, and Carlo. Carlo explained his situation and told the detectives he had to leave the country to facilitate the huge drug shipment. Once the plan was set he would contact my father with the details.

To seal the deal, and as a show of good faith, Carlo handed my father an envelope with $2000 in cash. My dad said he did not want it but Carlo insisted he take it. My father said, "*I am just holding this for you until you get back Carlo.*" This is where my father made a big mistake. Even though he did not want the money the fact that he took it proved to be a big part of his undoing.

He let Carlo go, and waited for his call. But the call never came. This would be the last time he would see or hear from Carlo.

I often think about how my father was feeling after this meeting. He was on the verge of cracking this huge case, and receiving the attention he so desperately desired. The overwhelming desire to receive this acceptance was intoxicating and overpowering.

Think about something you have always wanted in your life. Now, imagine you are watching it unfold in front of you. How would you feel being so close to a life-long dream? I can only imagine what was going through my dad's head.

This brings us to a few important questions.

» What do you want?

» How will you feel when you get it?

As you are chasing desires these questions should always be front and center. What are the feelings attached to these answers? It will tell you exactly where you are as you move forward in any area of your life.

Remaining balanced as you move toward your accomplishments is a critical part of the process. Being aware of how you are feeling is the tool you can use to maintain your balance. If you know how you really feel and can be honest, you will greatly increase your odds of success.

Awareness of your emotional state is a paramount issue in your personal development and growth. This awareness will allow you to catch yourself, and make the proper adjustments as you move forward.

My father did not have the awareness to avoid the perils of his chase. He was in too deep of a distortion to truly understand what was happening all around him.

I PROMISE YOU

7

As YOU CHASE, BE AWARE of the shiny object. It may come in the form of a promise or future opportunity. I experienced this many times as I was navigating my way through the corporate world of employment and advancement. One of my first jobs was a doorman at a New York City nightclub. I had applied as a bartender but there were no open positions at the time. The owner told me he had a position at the door, and as soon as the next bartender position became available it would be mine.

I took him at his word and worked at the door for almost a year. Finally, one of the bartenders was leaving and a position was now open. All my hard work and dedication was finally going to pay off. The owner hired a new bartender from the outside, and never said a word to me.

Even back then I was not the type of person to just sit back and let that happen. I confronted the owner regarding his promise to me. His answer was, *"you will get the next spot as soon as it becomes available Joe."* I quit on the spot.

This type of thing happened to me several times in my career. I was promised something which held me hostage. The real question to ask myself is, if I really wanted a bartender job, why did I accept the position at the door in the first place? I see it clearly now as a lack of confidence as this would have been my first bartending job. I accepted the first offer that came along based on my own insecurities.

Then there was the promise tied to my childhood. My father would promise me things all the time, and not deliver. All I did was play out this same event with different people. These patterns are prevalent in your behavior and desire to chase.

I remember a specific incident when I was around seven years old. My dad told me early in the week he was taking me to a New York Giants football game on Sunday. I was excited about this all week. When Sunday came, my dad went out with friends, and we never went to the game. This scenario played out many times and created a cycle of energy for me. I was used to someone promising me something and not delivering, being disappointed became a normal feeling for me.

This was tied to my chase and I played it out many times in my life. I kept on waiting for someone to come through and deliver what they had promised. I continued to attract people who were like my father in this area.

Have you been a victim of the promise? If so, look back into your childhood for answers. I guarantee you this is where you will find the root of your issue. It is easy to hold anger toward the people who have let you down. This is the first step in the healing process. You have the right to feel the anger.

Moving forward it is important to understand what you are attracting in this area. As you deal with the anger and disappointment you will no longer accept this type of behavior. In higher energy, you will not attract people who disappoint you.

Holding the negative feeling and judgment holds you in the space. Get mad, feel the pain, and let it go. My father did not consciously want to hurt me. He did what he wanted to do, and was not aware of my feelings. He was not capable of understanding the damage he was inflicting on me.

It still damaged me emotionally. I had to process those feelings by first accepting them and then allowing myself to feel the pain. As I felt the feeling and released the energy, my desire to feel disappointed dissolved.

I was always chasing the approval of these father figure types. They came in the form of bosses or people of higher status. I was waiting for their approval and acceptance as I never received it from my father, or any of these people who made promises to me.

Look to your internal insecurities and the desire to be accepted in this area of your life. If you have been or are being lured by *the promise* it is time to let it go. Many people use this as a tool to manipulate others. You will attract such people if this has been a part of your childhood and early life.

Do not project your anger on the person making the promise as they are only filling the role of your parents. Look to the core of the feeling and its origination. Deal with the feelings at the core level. This is the only way to let it go.

My father was always seeking acceptance, and he believed he would get it from Carlo in some way. Once again, he was looking in the wrong place. Carlo disappointed him and let him down as he had done with me. That karma always comes around. My father experienced the same feelings in his childhood with his own parents. He did not feel accepted or important.

The unfulfilled promise is tied to deep feelings of disappointment. As I opened this door I was flooded with emotion. Memories regarding incidents of promises and disappointments were overwhelming. It happened to me with coaches, friends, family, in relationships, and with bosses.

Once I was aware of this pattern, it completely changed my life. I could not believe how many times I had created the exact same scenario. I now realize, and accept, this was all created by me and the unresolved feelings I was holding. These unresolved emotional scars create our pain. You are here to have this emotional experience. Accept it as part of your journey and learn your lessons well.

MY FATHER'S CHASE COMES TO AN END

SOME TIME HAD PASSED, and there was no call from Carlo. My father was smart enough to know that his plan was headed south. This sent him into panic mode and he felt the walls closing in on him. By this time some heavy hitters from Washington, DC had been sent to New York. They were there to close out the sting operation, and give my father his options.

I remember him at that time sitting in a chair in the living room, completely disconnected from everyone else. He loved music, and would sit off in the corner of the room listening to his favorite albums with headphones. He sat there with a blank look on his face. It was a look of fear and despair. This was a man in trouble, who was now boxed into a corner. He went to see his attorney, a family friend named John. My dad gave John the $2000 he had received from Carlo and told him the story. As it all shook out John felt they did not really have much of case against him, he believed my father would probably be absolved of any charges based on a lack of substantial evidence. There might be a suspension, or in the worst case a dismissal from the police department.

A public humiliation for a person like my father was the ultimate disgrace. I can't imagine what he was feeling as this possibility swam around in his head. He was so prideful, and concerned about what everyone else thought of him, especially his mother, the woman he spent his life trying to impress. My father was extremely concerned about what others thought of him. This trait proved to be a big part of his undoing.

My father was called into a meeting with the guys from DC, and some of the top brass in the New York City Police Department. They offered him a deal. He was to become an informant within the police department. In this scenario, he would work with other detectives and report back their unethical behavior. My Dad would be setting up the guys he knew and trusted for many years.

This deal would solve all his problems. There would be no dismissal, no job loss, and no humiliation. All he had to do was agree to turn on his partners. It was presented in this manner- *you can take this deal, go to jail, or blow your brains out.* This was how one of my father's friends described the situation to me as a young adult.

I am not sure about the exact timeline of these events, as I was just a kid watching his father fall apart. He was always such a powerful figure in my life. To see him in this weakened and confused state was very disturbing.

In addition to the pressure from the police department my father was also being grilled by some of the underworld figures with whom he associated. As you would image these are not the most trusting or forgiving people.

These shady figures were concerned my dad would crack

under pressure and give them up as well. Now he was trapped between these two factions with nowhere to turn.

Even under all this pressure my dad was not willing to turn on his friends in the department. This placed him a very difficult situation. I am not sure how long he deliberated about his decision. As a 12-year-old, I was confused and uneasy about the situation.

On March 27, 1972, my father dropped my sister and me off at school. He was very quiet and focused. As I jumped out of the back seat of his unmarked police car I said, *"Have a good day Dad."* These were the last words I would ever say to my father.

He was heading into Manhattan for his meeting with the guys from DC. His partner Louis was going as well. Louis described my father as being in good spirits on the way to the meeting. He also told me that my father felt confident going in after his meeting with the attorney.

My father instructed Louis, who was driving, that on the way in he had to make a quick stop in Brooklyn. They drove to a desolate warehouse area near the Williamsburg Bridge just outside Manhattan. My father told Louis to stay in the car as he walked down the block.

There he met with two men who I assume to be underworld figures of some kind. When he returned to the car Louis described him as visibly shaken. He did not disclose any other information to me regarding the encounter. All I knew for sure was that something changed after his conversation.

My day progressed in a normal manner. The weather was beginning to break in New York. The warm sun bleached the street as I walked home from school. It was an exciting time as the new set of TOPPS baseball cards had come out and the season was just days away. My friend Mike and I looked through our new cards hoping to get a Yankee in the pack.

We arrived at my house which was in the middle of a steep hill in our suburban Queens neighborhood. It was a quiet tree lined street with Tudor homes on small lots of property. We had a long driveway and always used the side door as the main entrance. I was standing at the end of the driveway looking at my cards when the side door swung open. I was surprised to see my maternal grandfather, on my mother's side. This was odd because he worked and usually only came to visit on the weekend.

Although this was a strange occurrence, I was unfazed. I was happy to see him as we were very close. He told me to come inside using a stern voice. When I entered kitchen through the side door I could see something was wrong. There were people everywhere and I felt myself spinning. Suddenly I was in the living room when my mother grabbed me and said, *"Daddy went to heaven today."*

Everything stopped.

My father's chase was over. There would be no more big cases or visions of glory. There would be no book and movie deal. There would be no more family dinners or vacations. Now there was only a void.

My father was found dead in his unmarked car in Brooklyn just a few blocks from where he grew up. The death was deemed a suicide based on the fact he was shot with his own gun. Later, evidence came out that would dispute these findings but my mother never received his pension or any benefits from the police department.

There were many stories swirling around his case, but we never knew what happened. Some say he was killed, while others believed it was a suicide. I have made peace with the situation and moved forward. This emotional work has been the key to my healing process.

Losing a parent at any age is difficult. There are so many emotions and feelings swirling around inside you. As a 12-year-old I was not equipped to process what had occurred.

In life, we all face challenges and tragedies. How these situations are handled from an emotional perspective is extremely important, the impact of such an event leaves devastating emotional scars. This was not a time of therapy and counseling. My mother did not come from this type of background, and the idea of therapy, for herself or her kids, never entered her mind.

Her philosophy was very simple: bad things happen and you go on with your life. There was no room for grieving or processing any of the emotions created by this event. We stuffed our emotions and moved on.

Once again, we have the positive and negative impact of every situation. On the positive side, I became resilient and tough. On the negative side, I repressed all my feelings and continued to carry pain my entire life. Holding this type of energy creates a lot of issues in life...as you would imagine.

STEPPING INTO THE LIGHT

I was a very anti-spiritual person growing up which continued into my twenties. Like many people, I connected religion and spirituality. I was not a big fan of my Catholic upbringing which moved me away from anything in that realm.

My father passed when I was 12 in a violent incident. This event created a deep disconnect and feeling of abandonment for me. It was extremely painful, but in a strange way it was the beginning of my spiritual journey.

This single event dramatically accelerated my desire to chase, and created one painful event after another. My chase, like my father's, revolved around being successful. I was conditioned to be the responsible man of the house after my father's death. This feeling drove me to work at break-neck speed to create success as fast as possible.

I started working right after high school and by the time I was 19 I had purchased my first business. As you can see, I was in a big rush. I went through my first bankruptcy at the age of 20 and I bounced around for a while in various jobs including bartender and nightclub manager in New York City. I started another business at age 25, and went bankrupt again by 30. Talk about chasing your life.

I had an overwhelming feeling of pressure and responsibility that chased me for years. My belief was hard work is the answer. If I keep on working my ass off, things will eventually turn in my direction. As I approached the second bankruptcy, I realized this system was not working. I started with therapy, and later moved into energy work to begin my transformation.

Loss creates a feeling of abandonment and dramatically increases your desire to fill the void. All of us have experienced loss on some level. It comes in many forms including; divorce, illness, people moving away and financial hardship. All of these situations can create a feeling of loss in your life.

When you lose something, it is natural to make every effort to find or replace it. In this case, we are trying to find something, the feeling of inner self-love, we have never experienced. It is for this reason we are trapped in a never-ending chase. We are desperately trying to find something we have never had, and thus do not really know what we are seeking.

Imagine leaving your home every day, desperately looking for something you can never find. It is enough to drive you mad!

Now it is time to step off this track. Once again, this sounds easy, but you are now so addicted to the chase you cannot give it up. Somewhere deep in your mind you believe you can find it. This is the belief that holds you hostage. Giving up this belief is the key to setting yourself free.

As you begin the process of working on your inner-self you are stepping into the light. You are becoming enlightened. This is a process of many stages and layers. Each step you take brings you to a higher level of awareness and understanding. Once you jump on the enlightenment train, there is no turning back.

You will know and understand things from a completely different perspective. To accomplish this, you must be willing to challenge your current belief system. This is scary, as you begin to shatter many of the false truths you have been holding for many years. These beliefs are deep and many are buried in your unconscious mind. You will begin to uncover feelings and beliefs you did not know existed. Remain open to your findings to accelerate your process.

Moving into the light is an expansive experience. Your awareness is heightened, and your energy vibration changes. At this new level of higher energy you will gravitate to people and situations that are also in the light. You know what that means: you move away from people who are living in darkness. This is based on non-judgmental energy, not your sentiment. Many of the people living in the dark will be family and close friends. Energy does not make any exceptions or judgments. It simply seeks similar energy.

Your energy field does not say, *"That is my mother, father, sister or brother."* It simply responds based on what you are feeling. In this case, you are being pushed toward the light as your awareness is elevated.

Light and darkness cannot exist in the same place. You will be drawn to those who are in light or on the path to enlightenment. Those who choose to remain in the dark are not interested in bringing light to the area. The light does not discern who is who. You must accept the inevitable changes in your relationships as you walk this path.

CHASING TIME: YOUR PAST AND FUTURE

TIME ALSO PLAYS A ROLE in your chasing nature. When you are younger, you are chasing the future. As you get older, you are chasing the past. What were your beliefs, goals, and dreams? How idealistic were you about what your future held?

In youth, the chase represents what you think you want in life. In many cases this is tied to accomplishments in the physical world. A successful career, marriage and children are common goals. There are a chosen few who are blessed with a clear vision of exactly what they were placed here to do at a young age. I envy these people, as their path was presented to them so early. Most of us move through life's experiences and seek our true path. In some cases, people never get on this track and leave this planet feeling empty.

Your true purpose is coded to your soul. It is in your DNA, each person knows what they are here to do in this lifetime. The trick is reconnecting to what is already inside of you. This is a big part of our journey here in the physical world.

I want to take you on a journey, your journey to this point in your life. This exercise will help you understand yourself and your personal chase on a deeper level.

Revealing Your Chase Exercise: I suggest you write things down in a journal when doing this exercise. This process will help you see yourself and your journey in a more expansive way.

STEP 1: GOING BACK

Go back to your childhood, and remember yourself as a wide-eyed kid with millions of dreams regarding your amazing future. If you are unclear do not worry. Just stay with this process and your memories will come back.

What did you want to be and do with your life back then?

Write down as many things as you can regardless of how crazy they may sound to you right now. This will help you connect to your true purpose. It will also show you what was driving you at that time in your life.

STEP 2: MOTIVATION

Now, I am going to ask you to go a little deeper and connect to your emotions. The key to understanding your chase is based on what is emotionally driving you to move forward.

1-Why did you want X at that time?

2-What was driving you emotionally?

3-What was your desire?

4-What was the outcome?

Let's look at these questions, and how you answered them. Once again, being completely honest is the key to understanding yourself and your motivation.

Why did you want X at that time?

This is your why question. Where did this desire come from and what started you moving in that direction? I had a strong desire to be a successful businessman when I was younger. I never thought about where that desire came from until later in my life. I had many friends who were happy to finish college and get a job. I did not understand this idea and judged them for it back then.

As you go deeper the true feelings begin to emerge. These are some of the most common responses:

» To please your parents/family

» To feed your ego

» To be sensible

» To be safe and secure

» To be accepted

» To be admired

» To be appreciated

» To prove yourself

» To show others you were capable

» To be responsible

» To create: Give yourself a gold star if this was your answer

Most of these answers are based on what you learned and what was expected of you. Do not underestimate the expectations of your family, especially your parents. We are seeking approval and love. It makes perfect sense that you would do something to make your parents happy with the hope that you would receive the love you were seeking.

What was driving you emotionally?

Now it is time to understand what you were feeling at that time. This is a little tricky, as you move away from the mind and into your feelings. I am sure you could give me a list of logical answers for your decisions. In this case, we are looking for the emotion.

Connecting to the emotion is more challenging, as we have been conditioned to make logical decisions and take the safe road. When something does not make sense, people fear it. This is how inventors and creative people change the world. They are willing to go down the unknown road and see what happens.

What did you feel? In many cases, people begin by saying why they did it. That is not the question. I want to know how you were feeling about it.

How does the kid who wanted to be an artist feel when she goes to business school to make her parents happy?

Again, write it down. Did you feel excited, stressed, apathetic, fearful, compliant, resistant, blissful? This answer will help you gain a deeper knowing of who you were at that time.

What was your desire?

Your desire is tied to where you believe this path will take you in the future. You are chasing an imagined outcome you believe, or have been conditioned to believe, will make you happy.

What did you believe would happen in your life by taking this path? This is one you want to really sit with and ruminate on. Was this what you desired for your life? Many people are chasing a false desire based on what they have been conditioned to believe. In many cases, this is tied to an approval seeking behavior.

Did you follow your desire or acquiesce based on family pressure and circumstance?

What was the outcome?

» How did this chase end for you?

» Did you get what you wanted?

» If so, did it make you happy?

You see, it is common to get what you desired, and still feel unhappy in the end. I know what you are thinking: how can that be possible? Simple, you attached your happiness to an external accomplishment, relationship, career, amount of money, car, house, the list goes on.

I am not here to suggest you forgo all the benefits of the physical world. Just adjust your expectations and beliefs regarding the level of importance they hold.

As a young person, you have been conditioned to chase a desired future. There are certain beliefs you have been given through your family, friends, and society. When I was a kid, we were conditioned to get married, have kids, buy a house, and get a job with a good company that provides solid benefits. This is what I think of as the stability model. It is the safe road to take to create security.

Most of my friends, even those who took this path, ended up losing their jobs at some point. They were then challenged with reinventing themselves, or in some cases taking jobs for a lot less money in their forties and fifties.

Others married when they were very young to get a jump start on the kids and house. Once again, it worked well for some, and not so well for others.

There are no perfect answers here. The key is looking at your life right now and deciding what is the best course to take from this point forward. It is never too late to create the life you came here to live.

THE GOOD OLD DAYS

Another category is filled with those who peaked early. You know the child stars, high school quarterbacks, prom queens and those who had success early in life, but were unable to sustain it.

Many of these people are living in the past and hoping to return to those glory days. In some way, they are chasing the memories of the past instead of focusing on creating a better future.

When people are always talking about the good old days they have given up on the here and now. This may be your story but there are still more chapters to be written if you are willing to step out of the past and into the present.

REMOVING TIME FROM THE EQUATION

You can't change the past. Whatever happened, whatever decisions you made and outcomes you created are now part of your unique journey.

Don't label them as good or bad. These were experiences that shaped your character and made you who you are today. I always joke about all my ups and downs when I speak at events. I say that I needed these things to happen in my life to provide me with material for my presentations.

You are starting today from your current position. As I said earlier, the universe has a better plan than you do. You must believe this to move forward at the highest level. It is not about just saying the words.

Do you believe you are exactly where you are supposed be right now?

Once you accept this principle, your life will change dramatically. You have now removed one of the key negatives of the chase. Resisting where you are in life. Don't forget about the chapter on humans being malcontents. You will always desire more, but it is important to accept your current position to clear your path and move forward.

Acceptance adds speed to your journey.

Resistance stops you in your tracks.

Remove the issues of the physical world. How old you are, how tall you are, your gender, your ethnicity, your background, your education, your health. Simply remain present and start moving forward. This is when the miracles start to happen.

YOUR TRUST AND FAITH

10

AT SOME POINT, I knew I would have to address this part of your journey. In this case, I am referring to trusting the universe and having faith that everything will work out for your highest and greatest good.

The areas of trust and faith have been very challenging for me and many others I have encountered along this journey. The loss of my father had a big impact on my faith. It was hard for me, as a 12-year-old, to accept it. How was this something for my highest and greatest good? Not that I had any idea about this concept back then. Now, as I look back at my life, it all makes perfect sense to me.

Your struggle or ease regarding trust and faith is based on what you learned and your personal experience. I have seen very different feelings regarding this issue. People who have had an easy life have more faith and trust than those who have faced many challenges.

We have seen this phenomenon with people from all walks of life. I was watching an interview with character actor, Daniel Stern. You may not know the name but if you look him up you will recognize him right away. He talked about how things just worked out from the beginning and how he flowed from one part another. Then you have a guy like Jeremy Renner, who worked in the industry for over 20 years before he got his big break in The Hurt Locker.

In Stern's case, his experience gave him a lot of trust and faith in following his dream. Everything he did worked as he built his career. This validated his work and continued to move him forward. I am sure Renner faced many doubts as he struggled to make a living. It is difficult to have trust and faith when nothing seems to be working no matter how hard you try.

People like to find sensible reasons for everything, and this is an area that makes many want to pull their hair out. Why did everything flow for Stern, while Renner had to travel such a rough road? Why didn't Renner quit after years of hardship? This brings us to the topic of individual journeys, which I will address a little later.

As for trust and faith, when you struggle it is challenging to believe everything will work out in the end. You have no reason to believe because you have never seen it happen. All you have is your deep inner belief and dogged determination.

I have always been fascinated with successful people, and wanted to know how they built their businesses. This prompted me to begin reading biographies of successful entrepreneurs.

My list included Walt Disney, Ray Kroc, Howard Schultz, Mary Kay, and many others. In each case, these determined entrepreneurs faced monumental challenges in their quests for success. The question that came to me was this: what continued to drive these people forward after so much rejection and failure? Most people would have given up and walked away.

Each one had a common theme, they all believed deep-down that sooner later they would succeed. I often wondered where this belief and faith came from, based on the results they had seen before succeeding. It was an inner feeling of faith and knowing. This is the inner voice deep in your soul pushing you forward.

How do you remain faithful when you have had such a difficult time in life? How do you trust people when so many have let you down?

I know I sound like a broken record, but it goes back to being in acceptance. When you accept your journey, things begin to flow and life becomes easier. You cannot be in a state of trust and faith when you are resisting your life. I am not saying you should start trusting everyone you meet. The key is being open to the possibility of attracting better people and opportunities... Believe!

Another issue is feeling you are pushing a boulder up hill. It is one thing to be dedicated and work hard. It is another to feel overwhelming resistance every step of the way. It is time to give up your desire to struggle. You have been conditioned to struggle and it has been a part of your journey. It is no longer necessary to hold on to this feeling.

Chasing energy is negative and fear based. Flowing energy is positive and love based. The energy is completely different, and the results are predetermined.

HONORING YOUR STRUGGLE

We can all accept some struggles in life, but after a while these failures take a toll. I was one of these people who struggled at every level. There were a few temporary high points but most of the time I struggled to move forward. I wore this as a badge of honor for many years. At no point, did I accept the pain of my struggle.

I was trained and conditioned to be a good soldier. You keep moving forward and never complain. I held all the pain and heartache of my struggle. My early experiences made me resilient and tough. I was a true warrior and had the ability to bounce back. These traits are good in some cases, and not so good in others.

When I finally broke, there was an explosion of emotion. I had finally allowed myself to grieve the pain and heartache of my struggle. I was not giving up. It was a cleansing experience as I cried for hours and released the pain I had stuffed down for years.

There was a very important element to this release of energy. At no point did I feel like a victim. This allowed me to feel the intensity of the emotion without judgment. You cannot clear your energy feeling like a victim. As a victim, you project the pain and use outside circumstances to validate your situation.

This was a true emotional experience without blame or pity. In this state, you are able to allow yourself to let go of the emotions that are holding you back and lowering your vibration of energy.

There is nothing wrong with breaking down every now and then. It is a great way to cleanse your soul and lighten your load.

WHAT ABOUT WORK?

Your willingness to do the inner work is a critical piece of your journey. Many believe, once I know what I want to do everything will flow. That may be the case, to a degree, but there is always work involved. Creation takes work, and you are here to create.

Here's how it works: you were given certain skills based on your mission in this lifetime. What you do with those skills is up to you. Will you work hard to improve, or will you slack off?

People in life who are great at anything have worked hard regardless of skill level. Gifted people who work hard become the greatest in their field of endeavor. Then we have the less gifted who work even harder to become very good, and in some cases great in their field of endeavor.

We have all seen this in our own lives. How many kids did you grow up with who were exceptional students or great athletes? What happened to them? I am sure you will say some were very successful, and others didn't go too far. If you look a little deeper you will see those who worked and followed through were successful.

My first book was titled *No More 9 to 5*. Back then I was teaching people how to start a business from home while they still had a job, as I had done. One of the segments focused on the work, commitment, and mindset necessary to succeed. In some cases, people would come up to me at the end of the class and say, *"Thank you, I now know this is not what I want to do."*

I was devastated. I thought my presentation was too strong, and that I had killed their dream. One evening a gentleman who made this type of comment stayed after the class to talk. He was thanking me for all the help. I said, *"What help? You told me you're not moving forward."* He replied, *"Joe you helped me understand myself and know the career path I want to take, and it is not one of an entrepreneur. I am forever grateful to you for this session."*

This shattered another belief of mine, one that life was about being in your own business. I then realized this is not the path for everyone. It is about creating and this can take many forms.

Regardless of the road you choose, be ready to roll up your sleeves and dive into the mission you have selected. Ask yourself, how do I become the best? By 'best' I am referring to being your best-self. The term best is subjective and at the heart of many great debates. Who was the best actor, writer, baseball player, scientist, and so on? There is no right or wrong answer here. It is all about knowing deep-down that you are being your best.

Your best-self today is not going to be your best tomorrow. Each day, we have the opportunity to evolve and grow. When you choose growth, you are always getting better. Don't worry about what anyone else is doing as it has no impact on you. Your job is simple, be your best every day.

TRUST, FAITH, AND ATTRACTION

As you begin to clear your energy (using the exercises in Chapter 5) things will begin to shift. I was always attracting people who promised me opportunities and then backed out. This was tied to my energy, and the disappointment I experienced as a child.

After some energy work, it took a while, I started to attract different people and better situations. At first I was apprehensive regarding these opportunities. My natural defenses were up, being born and raised in New York didn't help. "Why are these people being so nice to me?" I often wondered.

Building, or should I say rebuilding, your trust and faith takes time. You may have become accustomed to deception, disappointment, and struggle. Someone helping you or presenting a new opportunity may seem strange at first.

Take a moment to evaluate your current levels of trust and faith. Each person will be in a different place based on background and life experience. Answer quickly without much thought for the best results and most honest answers.

TRUST AND FAITH EXERCISE

(Answer these questions on a scale of 1-10, 10 being the best)

1. Do you believe people are true to their word?

2. How much do you trust your family (parents, siblings)?

3. How much do you trust your close friends?

4. How much do you trust your romantic partner?

(If you are not currently in a relationship use your most recent experience)

5. Do you believe good things will happen in your life?

Total

The best score you could have is 50, which is pretty much impossible. This is not a test. Your score is designed to show you how your trust and faith was developed. The first four questions are tied to trust. Most, if not all of your trust issues, will be tied back to your parents. If you could not trust them, who could you trust?

The energy you are carrying regarding trust goes all the way back to the emotions of your childhood. A fear, or lack of trust in others, carries forward. In this energy, you continue to attract people you cannot trust. This validates your belief and holds you in the same cycle. Your ego loves to be right, and by continuing to attract the same people and situations you continue to validate this belief.

People who grew up in a safer, more trusting environment have more belief and trust. They tend to attract more positive people and situations to reinforce the belief that people can be trusted. This is the amazing thing about energy work, you are always attracting based on what you feel and believe, not what you think.

It is always good to remain cautious, as trust is something people earn over time. As your energy improves you will begin to attract in a different way. This will help you gain more trust moving forward.

Question five is about your faith. Do you believe positive things will happen in your life? It is easy to say yes, but you must feel it deep in your soul. Based on past struggles, it can be difficult to have faith.

Why should I believe my relationships, career or health will improve now? You might think, I have been working on this for years and have never created the results I desire? I hear answers like this every day and I agree. It is challenging to move into faith when there is nothing happening to make you believe things will improve. This was one of the most difficult areas for me for many reasons. It started with my results. I had worked hard for years, and all I had to show for it was two bankruptcies and a ton of heartache.

I never thought about faith or trust, because to me success was all about working hard and being determined. Why did I need faith or trust? All I had to do was work my plan to succeed. I was not aware at the time, but I was chasing success because it was how I was going to gain the respect and love I desired. This was a negative, fear-based desire which showed up in my results.

Working from a position of trust and faith is completely different. In this energy, you are not chasing you are trusting. You have faith that you are always being directed for your highest and greatest good. There is no reason to chase anything from this perspective.

When you let go of the desire to chase, you have a different feeling inside. The fear driving the chase is gone. You are replacing fear with faith. It is an amazing transition, and it takes time to reach this place.

Having faith is a feeling. It is not something you can manufacture. I always wanted to have faith and tricked myself into believing I had it. When I searched my feelings, I knew it was not there. Maybe a little here and there but I did not have true belief.

This was something I always wanted but could never create. When it happened one day, without warning, the emotion was palpable. I felt inner peace and knew everything was going to be okay. Having faith is one of the keys to ending your chase. When you surrender your desire to chase your faith will take over.

HOW DID THIS HAPPEN?

In your new energy, opportunities will appear out of thin air. You will ask yourself, how did this happen? I didn't do anything to create this opportunity. This is not true, because shifting your energy and beliefs is doing something. It is inner work, which many do not see as doing something.

Most of us have been taught we must do A to get B. When something positive comes in unexpectedly it is a big surprise. Then your mind jumps in and asks, how did that happen? You want to know how you did it so you can do it again.

Now you know you created it with your energy. It may not have come in the form you expected, and that may throw you off. This is the magic of positive attraction. You are attracting things into your life on an unconscious level 24/7. When something negative happens, it is important to know you brought it in for a reason.

At a higher level of awareness, you know it is not good or bad. I keep beating this drum, because this is how you move out of judgment. Be aware of what you are attracting all day. This will help you gauge your energy, and adjust on the spot. If you are having an off day, take a moment to stop and take a few deep breaths to reset your day. Stop, and focus on what you want to create.

Also, take notice of your feelings and emotions when you attract things you deem undesirable. These are the unresolved emotions and feelings you will work on to move forward. Every encounter is a gift when you see it from this perspective.

You are creating opportunities all the time. Your ability to see them and optimize those opportunities will accelerate your process dramatically. Every adjustment takes you to a higher place. You will build momentum and move faster as you continue to make positive changes.

HOW IS YOUR KARMA?

11

WE ALL KNOW PEOPLE who have lives that seem to be easy and flowing. Why is this happening for them and not me? There are many ways to answer this question. Based on my work with karma and energy, I will give you my answer to this perplexing question.

Each person comes to this planet with a karmic map (I discussed this in my book *Karma Buster*). You have specific things you came to experience on an emotional level. All experiences here on earth are tied to your emotions. Your soul came to have a unique experience, and your friends with an easier life came to have a different experience.

You chose your experience in this lifetime before you arrived here on earth. This is the reason some people have easier lives than others. They came to have an easy life and you came to expand yourself to a higher level. Not better or worse just different. Those of us on a spiritual journey usually chose a more challenging path. This is how we experience the full spectrum of emotions at the highest level. More issues equal more emotions and more emotions create a deeper experience. The more you are challenged, the more you grow as a person.

As you move forward it is important to embrace your unique journey. You take the good along with the bad. In spiritual work, there is no good or bad. Humans feel compelled to place a judgment on everything. We label it as good, bad, positive, negative, right, wrong. Moving forward, it is better to remove the judgment. It is what it is and that is the end of it.

The key to moving forward is understanding each experience on an emotional level. When you see things from this perspective everything changes. To accomplish this feat, you must step away from what is happening in the physical or third dimensional world.

I know what you are thinking, "How do I do that?"

Let me give you an example and a technique I have been using and teaching for many years. I call it "Stepping Out." This is an example of how to use this technique. Let's say you are in an argument with a friend or family member. Those things happen in life, after all. Most of those disagreements are based on ego and point of view. You see it one way, and they see it another way.

Your ego has a very strong desire to win and be right. Once you are in an ego-state you have disconnected from your higher-self. Now you are in a full scale third dimensional battle of wills. Most of the problems we see in the physical world are based on egos and the desire to win and be right.

Moving forward requires you to see things from a higher perspective. Instead of engaging in a battle of egos you will rise above it. This is how you "Step Out" of the situation. When there is a disagreement or argument you step out of your ego and imagine yourself floating above the situation. You are looking down at yourself. In this case, you become the observer instead of the combatant.

Ask yourself, what is really happening here? Why are we fighting? Am I desperate to make my point and win?

I remember an argument I had with my mother about not attending a family function because I had other plans. She could not accept the fact that I would not be attending. I was desperately attempting to plead my case to get her to understand and accept my situation. My mother was in an ego-state, as was I, all she cared about was winning and getting me to change my plans and attend the function. I was desperately attempting to get her to see my side of it.

We went back and forth until the call ended without resolution. This caused friction and damaged our relationship. As I viewed this from a higher position, I knew this was a significant shift in our relationship. This situation had occurred many times in the past and I always acquiesced. I was ready to step into power and had to accept the fact that I was unable to make this work.

It was always my desire to keep the peace in the family. That desire stopped me from doing what was best for myself. After years of behaving the same way it was a shock to my mother when I changed the dynamic. I knew what I was doing and she did not. This was the reason for the conflict. I had changed the game, and my mother was not aware of the new rules.

Use the *Stepping Out* technique every time you encounter a challenging situation. You may not be able to *Step Out* on the spot in the beginning. In time, you will be able to transcend the situation and understand what is happening on an emotional soul level.

When you decide to step into power you are going to ruffle some feathers. You are breaking a family dynamic that has lasted for generations, in some cases. As you take your own path you are breaking old karmic cycles and family pathology.

As you clear energy, your desire to stay on your old path begins to dissolve. This is also tied to the identity you have been holding your entire life. You are now transitioning from your false-self to your true-self.

Living in the physical world requires you to have an identity. When you come here you separate from the oneness of source energy and take on an individual identity. This is necessary to have an experience here in the physical or third dimensional world.

Your unique identity is tied to your karmic journey and emotional mission. This is called the ego-identity because it is part of your false-self. Your true-self is all love and connected to source energy. We are here to have an emotional experience, which is why we take on a physical body. To have an emotional experience we must have polarity. This comes in the form of the opposite emotions and feelings we experience: happy or sad, love or fear, joy or sorrow.

You would not know the feeling of joy without the feeling of sorrow. If your whole life was filled with only joy, there would be no other feelings to experience. Accept all feelings and emotions as part of your experience.

GOING WITH THE PROGRAM

THIS IS THE PART WHERE I ask you to relax and go with the flow. This was, and still is at times, one of the most challenging areas for me. Another one of those phrases you have heard a million times, *just go with the flow.* As a driven person, I always struggled with the concept of sitting back and letting things happen. In my ego-state I was always trying to force things to create what I desired.

Let's consider it and examine this principle on a deeper level. Nature is our best example of going with the flow here on earth. It simply happens in divine order. Plants grow, seasons change, leaves fall and ocean waves continue to crash the beach.

Humans have been fighting nature from the beginning, and as you know nature always wins in the end. You can attempt to swim against the current and may succeed for a while but eventually the current wins.

The question here is, why are we constantly fighting against the current? Wouldn't it be easier to just relax, and go with it? I know what you're thinking: "How do I accomplish something in my life when I just sit back, and wait for it to show up?"

Sitting around and waiting is not what I am suggesting. Let's go back to man and nature. In the beginning, humans used their bodies to swim. Then we invented boats which were more efficient. They could carry more people and move faster than a person swimming. In this case, we enhanced the flow by creating a tool to use it more efficiently. This is also the case with communication. First, we spoke to each other, then we carved images on cave walls, and now we can speak to someone anywhere in the world using a small device we carry in our pockets.

The idea here is to blend your desires with the flow of energy. Your desire to chase creates a problem in this situation. You have a goal, and want to accomplish it as fast as possible. I think of this as the ego's calendar. You know what you want and you want it now. You are like a little kid who wants a cookie before dinner. The universe has a different schedule designed for your highest and greatest good. You are on a path, but there are things you must learn and discover before you move forward. Your ego does not like this idea, as it believes you should have it now.

Your highest and greatest good is based on the big picture. If you could see your entire life this would make more sense. We are only seeing what is directly in front of us. The idea that I need this challenging experience for my overall development can be difficult to digest.

There is also the matter of timing. Energy is always moving and things are happening that you cannot see. The right person, situation, idea, or meeting is being lined up in perfect order. The problem is, you are not aware of all this action. To you nothing is happening and it is driving you crazy. Just keep moving forward and hold the energy of creation. Good things happen when you remain in this space.

I experienced this when I was working on my book *Spiritual Selling*. I had been working on it for a while and was ready to have it published in 2006. Everyone told me I needed an agent. No major publisher will talk to you without an agent was the word from the so-called experts. I pursued an agent for some time without any positive results. They all told me the same thing, *"I only represent authors who have been published."* This is like banks who only give loans to people who don't need the money.

Realizing this was not working, I decided to send proposals directly to publishers myself. I received plenty of rejection letters. Throughout the entire process, I was only focused on getting the word out. My desire was to help create a shift in the business world. Finally, after almost a year without progress I decided to self-publish the book. I started to research the process and move in that direction.

A few weeks later I was on the phone with a colleague. He asked me what I was working on and I told him my *Spiritual Selling* story. His replied, *"Hey, Joe, I know a guy at Wiley and I think they would be interested in this topic."* He sent me the contact information for high level person at this major publisher.

I reached out immediately and set up a call. We spoke for a while, he was interested and asked me for a proposal. Within three weeks I had a deal, contract, and advance to write the book. My first thought was, how in the world did this happen so easily? There was no tension or force, just flow. What I came to realize was, I had a different feeling. I moved from a chasing feeling to a heart-felt desire feeling. My focus was getting the word out to help people. In the past, it would have been more ego driven. The book would have been more about prestige and personal accomplishment.

When the right opportunities show up it is important to follow through and act. Believe it or not, this is a step many people miss. It seems so obvious but there are unconscious fears and beliefs that can jump in and stop your progress.

There have been many occasions where I have given someone a contact that could help them. It could be for a job, business opportunity or just advice. When I see this person months later and ask them, *"How did it go?"* They say, *"Well I never got around to calling them, I am still in the same job."*

I have seen this so many times and it always takes me by surprise. People say they desire a certain thing in life. It could be a relationship, career opportunity or invitation to meet the perfect contact. Although this is something you desire there is always a fear of the unknown. You are about to step into a new world. Then the questions start coming up:

» Am I smart enough?

» Do I have the experience?

» Can I handle the responsibility and pressure?

» Will people like what I am offering?

» Will I be accepted?

» Will I be criticized?

These are some of the thoughts and feelings you will experience.

In your conscious mind, this makes no sense. This is the opportunity you have been waiting for your entire life. The question is, why wouldn't you jump on the opportunity you have been waiting for all this time? The simple answer is fear. Your deepest and darkest fears are going to come up now. All of your insecurities and doubts will show up in force. The key here is how you react and deal with these emotions.

We have been conditioned to deal with fear in two ways: run from it or push through it. I will suggest you simply accept it. This goes back to the acceptance or resistance concept I discussed earlier. The fear exists and that's fine. When you run from the fear, it grows. If you push forward you are attempting to act as if the fear does not exist. This may work for a while, but your unresolved issues are still there. Eventually, these emotions will show up again and create another issue.

When you accept the feeling of fear, you release the charge of energy it holds. You are no longer pushing against it. Acceptance dissolves the feeling and allows it to run though you. This will result in a sense of calmness. You may still have some anxiety, which is normal with any new experience, but the feeling of fear will be gone. This is how you replace fear with faith. It is a simple matter of full acceptance of all your emotions.

IT HAPPENED AGAIN

I had the same experience with this book. I was working on it for a few years and was ready to get the message out. This time around, I had an agent who was shopping the book for me, now I was a published author and had an agent. Getting a publisher should be a snap based on conventional wisdom.

Once again, no one was interested in the book. I was laughing to myself about these results. Now I had everything in place, and it wasn't working. Once again, I knew it was about the energy and the timing was not right. I fired my agent and kept working on finishing the book.

A few months later I reconnected with a friend I had not spoken to in over five years. She connected me to this publisher. Amazing, isn't it?

Easy and flowing as the timing and energy aligned. I also realized this was not the right agent for me. The universe made sure this did not work out as we were not meant to work together. This was not a good or bad thing, it was an energy thing. My energy was not aligned with this agent. I was protected from making a deal that would not have been for my highest and greatest good.

The big difference in these cases was my state of flow. I was moving in a direction but not chasing the outcome. I was focused on what I was creating and the universe took care of the details. This is a great place to be and you want to make it your home.

As you would imagine, this is easier said than done. When things do not seem to be progressing, as your ego would like, there is a tendency to start pushing. Your level of discomfort is tied to your ability to remain patient. This has been another tough lesson for me. I have always been a "go out and get it" type of person. The idea of sitting back is not in my DNA.

As a goal-oriented person, you may struggle with the concept of waiting. We have been trained to go after what we want. It is important to know when to act and when to step back which is tied to your feelings. Before you act, take your emotional temperature. Are you acting out of fear? If the answer is yes, you know it is not the time to take action. Take a breath here and relax. All actions taken out of fear are sure to create negative results.

Be aware of your feelings and be sure to act based on love. When you are aligned, and flowing this will become easier. Learning to be patient takes practice and of course...patience.

Here is an exercise to help you gain a better perspective and help you become more patient and relaxed.

YOUR SERENDIPITY LIST

One day, I was sitting around feeling depressed. Things in my life were not working no matter how hard I tried. I was completely frustrated with my results and could not understand why this was happening.

Then I started to make a list of all the good things that happened in my life. My list included everything from getting an autograph at a baseball game to meeting my wife. I noticed that all these positive experiences seemed to just happen. They were organic in nature. I also realized that I was not thinking about anything. It was a case of being in the moment and flowing with the situation.

Make a list of all the great things that have come into your life. Once you get rolling, things will start popping into your head. Old memories from childhood of great experiences long forgotten, job opportunities that came your way, people you met who helped you along your journey.

You will see how these wonderful events flowed right to you. Bring yourself back to this state of flow. It takes time and practice to make this the space you live in. Your mind loves to jump in and create chaos. When you are flowing, you are not really thinking. This is a higher state of energy. I see it as conscious transcendence. Your physical body is here but your energy is in a higher place.

Remain aware and practice, practice, practice.

Eventually you will move into a constant state of flow and peace.

THE GREATER GOOD 13

YOUR DESIRE TO CHASE is tied to your ego. As you elevate your energy, this desire begins to fade, and is replaced with a new feeling. At a higher level of energy and aware-ness you realize we are all one. Whatever you do impacts every-one in the world. I know this may seem a bit overwhelming to grasp. I know what you are thinking: *"Joe if I do a good deed for my neighbor that ripple of energy impacts the entire world?"*

In our limited view, we see ourselves as small and in many cases, insignificant. How can my simple kind act make a difference? Let me help you expand your outlook and in the process your sense of power.

Our world population is around seven billion people right now. What would happen if one billion people woke up this morning in a state of peace and joy? They would share that energy with others and the feeling would begin to spread. It would continue to grow until this feeling effected every person in the world. You may see this as an idealistic vison, but I don't. To me this is the world we are in the process of creating right now.

You must understand, energy is non-judgmental. We have seen hate and negativity spread throughout the world on many occasions. This is also a form of energy. If hate can be spread why can't love?

Until now, this has been a challenge, because we have seen ourselves as separate individuals. Each person in an ego-state is only concerned with their own well-being. They are fear-based, and see the world through the eyes of an individual. In this state of fear, people are driven by their own agenda and the desire to get ahead of the pack. We see this every day in business, politics, school, families, and every other aspect of life. Many people are focused on personal gain above all.

At a higher level of awareness, you realize we are all in this together. Helping each other is the key to creating the world we truly desire. This brings us to the concept of the "Greater Good." From this perspective, you are making decisions that are good for the collective. Be aware that one of the people who benefits is you. This is not about self-sacrifice or becoming a martyr. The concept of the "Greater Good" includes everyone.

This may sound easy, but there are challenges in every situation. Let's say you are running a business and have 500 employees. Based on changes in the market you realize you are going to have to cut costs to keep the company going. The solution is laying off 100 people to save the other 400 jobs and the business.

The decision for the greater good is saving the 400 jobs and keeping the company solvent. Unfortunately, 100 people lose their jobs and must go back out to seek other employment. This may be the motivation they needed to start a business or pursue a bigger dream? In a perfect world, which we are not in, every decision would be easy and benefit everyone. In our world, this is more challenging.

We have seen major corporations make decisions that are strictly tied to the bottom-line and profits. In many of these cases there was not much, if any, consideration of the big picture. Looking at the impact of each decision and how it effects people is critical if we are to evolve as a species.

Going forward, I ask you to examine each decision you make and ask yourself this simple question: Is this decision for the Greater Good?

The idea here is to consider everyone and everything before making your decision. As we know, it is impossible to make everyone happy. Jesus couldn't do it, Gandhi couldn't do it, and Buddha couldn't do it; what chance do you have of doing it? You want to accept this truth and walk a path that feels good to you. As you move into this place of acceptance you realize it is impossible to please everyone. Being okay with this principle is important as you move forward.

Many years ago, I had a session with a trance-medium. These are people who can move into a trance like state and connect with higher level beings. You can ask any questions you desire about your life or the world in general. At the end of the session my question was, *"What are we here to do?"*

I sat back waiting for a profound, detailed answer. This was going to be the information that changed my life forever.

Bob, the trance-medium said, *"Well, you just want to leave the planet in better shape than you found it."*

At first I was disappointed with this simplistic answer. I was waiting for the wisdom of the universe and I get this basic statement.

As I pondered his response I realized the brilliance in the simplicity. What would the world look like if every person on earth had this objective? I have been contemplating this statement almost every day for the last 20 years.

I always check myself against this statement, and want to be sure I am constantly making the world a better place. I realize that every word I say or write, every interaction I have with another person, every thought and feeling makes a difference.

Live in this state of service and know you have the power to help heal the world. No individual can do it because we are all one. Elevate yourself and by doing so you are elevating others.

Keep the "Greater Good" in your awareness at all times and you will change the world.

SURRENDER IS NOT GIVING UP

MOVING FORWARD IN PEACE will require you to give up your chase. Many people see this as quitting. Nothing could be further from the truth. In this case, you are going to surrender your chase and let go of the frantic feeling you have been holding on to your entire life.

Words are very powerful, as they all carry vibration and strong associations. When you think of the word surrender what comes to mind? For many it is putting up the white flag and bowing down to an enemy.

Everything is a matter of context and perspective. In this case surrender is letting go of something that has caused you great pain and suffering. Your chase has been at the heart of so much pain and heartache. Doesn't it make sense to let this pain go?

Once again, fear plays a major role in this transition. What will happen when you stop chasing? You have been chasing your entire life and suddenly you just stop. What do you do now?

The answer is...Nothing!

That's right, a big fat nothing.

I know you may be freaking out right now because the concept of nothing is beyond your comprehension. When I think of the idea of nothing, it always reminds me of the Seinfeld Show. This is the show starring and created by Jerry Seinfeld and Larry David.

The entire premise was: This is a show about nothing.

In one episode Jerry and his friend George have a meeting with the NBC Network to pitch a show idea. Before the meeting, George emphatically expresses his opinion. He says, *"Everyone is doing something but we are doing nothing."*

Seinfeld went on to become one of the most successful shows in television history. Could you image walking in to a major network with the idea for a show about nothing? Once again, we have brilliance in simplicity.

We have been trained and conditioned to believe we must do something to get something. I encounter this constantly with clients and at live events. The belief is deeply engrained in our minds and hearts.

This goes back to Newton's Third Law: Every action has an equal and opposite reaction.

When you do something, something happens. Although this is true we tend to see it as it applies to physical action only. You go out, do something and there is a reaction. Can you also create an action by making an internal emotional shift? The answer, of course, is yes!

As a sales-trainer I have applied this principle many times in the world of business, where it is all about the numbers and accomplishments. At my first job, I was told I had to make 100 outbound calls per day to be successful. This was my first sales position and I had no idea what I was doing so I made 100 outbound calls per day. I had mixed results, as did many others in the office.

I also noticed the most successful people in the company were not making 100 calls per day. If this was the action necessary to succeed why were these individuals able to prosper without this step?

I have tested these, this is what you have to do theories, many times over the years. As I moved into energy work my perspective changed. I began to see things in a whole new way. One of my clients was a mortgage broker. She was a real dynamo and ultimate chaser named Janet. The chasing system had been successful for her career. It did create a lot of stress and some physical issues but she was willing to deal with it to be successful.

When the deals were slow in coming and business dropped she reached out to me for help. Janet was open to trying something new. My book *Spiritual Selling* had just come out and she was intrigued with the concept.

"I am doing exactly what I have always done, and nothing is working," she sighed. This was very frustrating for a person who had always been able to create business. She was working on a big deal when we met. All the presentations were made and the perspective client had all the information. A few weeks passed and no call. Janet was having a nervous breakdown. She was not used to waiting this long for an answer.

I asked her my favorite question, "How are you feeling?"

She replied, *"Nervous, anxious and annoyed."* I then asked, *"Do you feel you have done everything in your power to make this deal?"* Her emphatic reply was: YES!

My answer, *"There is nothing else you can do. It is time to surrender and trust the universe. If you are meant to have this deal you will have it."* Her head looked like it was going to explode as I uttered these words. I could see her blood pressure rising as each second passed.

Janet finally agreed to surrender and let it go. This is a two-step process:

Step 1: You mentally agree to let it go (this is the easier step)

Step 2: You let it go emotionally

It is easy to say you are letting go but feeling it emotionally is an entirely different issue. This is what happens every time people are not honest with how they feel. You may feel angry but you don't want to accept it.

You try to convince yourself you are not angry but you are still holding the energy and emotion. The question is, how do you let it go emotionally? This is an emotional release that happens inside you. It cannot be manipulated or controlled.

In most cases, it takes time to move from the mental aspect to the emotionally transformation. Your mind keeps jumping in trying to figure things out or come up with a solution.

Weeks passed and no call came in. On many occasions, Janet was tempted to reach out but held back and waited. After three long months, she broke down emotionally. She accepted the situation and let go of the expectation and desired outcome. "I don't care what happens anymore," was her comment. There was a palpable feeling as these words were spoken. Her surrender was finally complete. She accepted the fact that the deal was dead. Two weeks later the phone rang with good news, the deal was hers.

Although the work was done in the external world, this was an emotional experience for my client. She had to learn to relax and surrender. When she let go, her energy was completely different. There was no feeling of anxiety, stress, or pressure. This was a true internal transformation from chasing to surrendering.

In this case, there was an action that created a reaction. The difference here was, it was not a physical action. This was an emotional action or as I like to see it, transformation. Her energy changed and then the results shifted. Janet's surrender removed the tension and opened the door for her to receive.

There is no reason to wait months, or in some cases years, to surrender your pain. You can let it go right now. I know it all seems to be so easy but there are emotional factors at play. Do not underestimate your desire to hold on to your old identity. You have been conditioned over many years to see yourself in a certain way. Giving up that identity is a powerful shift.

As I said earlier, you require an identity to play here on earth. Our journey here is letting go of the false-self and connecting to your true-self. Knowing your ego-identity or false-self will help you move forward.

Your identity is tied to who you think you are supposed to be. Some of these traits are inherent in your DNA. Others are learned and developed as you grow up. Your environment, birth order, gender, race, family values, religion, and geographic location help in the development of your false-self.

Dissolving Your Identity: Search your feelings, and make a list of your traits and beliefs. For example, you believe you must work very hard to make a living. This belief is now part of your identity. Because you believe this, you are holding and vibrating the energy. You then go out and attract this reality which validates this belief in your mind. Now your ego-identity is happy because you have trapped yourself in this space.

You will see how your life is a direct reflection of these traits and beliefs. As you bring these to light and let them go your energy begins to shift and you start attracting better opportunities and people.

It is the same two-step process: First you agree to let it go, then you emotionally let it go. The emotional part is more challenging, because you are giving up a piece of yourself. You may not like it but it is how you see yourself. What happens when you give up the struggle and life becomes easier? I know it sounds good, but there is an emotional shift that must take place.

You hold the negative, painful identity because it is so comfortable. Allow yourself to give it up, cry it out, mourn the death, grieve the old you. This is how you gain freedom from your pain and suffering.

Your ego-identity wants to keep you small. Your higher-self wants you to be incredibly powerful. Every time you choose your higher-self you are elevating to a higher place and becoming more powerful.

I CAN'T SEE IT

As humans, we have a difficult time with things we cannot see. Your energy shifts, but you can't see it. The external changes do not take place immediately. How do you know it's working? We are coming back to faith. Beyond faith, you can tell by your internal feelings. As I do the work on my own energy, I know when there is a change in the way I feel. It may take some time to manifest in the physical world but you know something is changing inside.

It is not necessary to have physical action to create what you desire. You are always creating your life based on your feelings and beliefs. The external actions you take are secondary to your emotions. Continue to take actions that are aligned with your purpose and beliefs. Do not be afraid to stop and do nothing at times. This is how you create space for the universe to bring you new ideas, resources, and opportunities.

Surrender is tied to trust. In this high state of energy, the opportunities will find you. There is no reason to chase. You just keep moving forward and follow your gut instincts.

WITHDRAWAL SYMPTOMS

Giving up the chase is the same as letting go of any addiction. In the beginning, you will experience withdrawal symptoms. Stopping your chase is a major life change, and an adjustment period is required.

The key here is being very aware of your feelings and desires. You will feel the desire to chase when things are not progressing fast enough. This was the most difficult part for me, personally. When this happened, it brought up many emotions. I remember thinking, "How can I just sit around and goof off when nothing is happening."

Once again, I had to trust the universe, and know the plan for my life was perfect. As you would imagine there were good and bad days with this process. Some days I felt light and flowing. Then there were times when my skin was crawling and I was losing my mind. My daily morning meditation was a big help, as was my journaling. Exercise is also an excellent way to burn off some of the anxiety you may experience.

The more I held this peaceful, non-chasing space, the easier it became. I was transforming from the inside out and I could feel the changes occurring in me. My early days of discomfort and stress shifted to peace, trust, and faith.

One of the greatest lessons I learned in this process was divine timing. As I have stated many times in this book, energy is always moving. The universe is always working for your highest and greatest good. It is setting things up for you in divine order. All elements must be aligned properly before you move to the next adventure of your journey. You may feel you are ready, but believe me when I say the universe knows better.

LOOK FOR VALIDATIONS

The universe is constantly sending us messages. I think of these as breadcrumbs along my path, little things that tell us if we are on course or need a slight adjustment.

These validations come in many forms. They can be found in dreams, music, movies, books, a billboard, or a comment someone makes to you. We have all had the experience of thinking of a person, and then they call you. You may pass this off as a coincidence, but it is a psychic event. Ideas and thoughts do not just enter your awareness for no reason.

You are constantly receiving messages, but most people are not aware enough to realize it. Some are obvious, while others are subtle. The more you tune in, the easier it will be. Your awareness and connection to your higher-self is the key here.

I remember a time when I was thinking about moving from

New York to California. It was something that ran through my mind, but I never told anyone about it. A few weeks later I went to check my mail and I found a large envelope. A friend had sent me a book of homes in Southern California. Did he read my mind? A few years later we did move to the Golden State. Be aware of these messages especially when they follow a thought. These are very powerful validations and they will help you keep your journey flowing.

On many occasions, I have asked for specific guidance. When I am confused or not sure about something I like to reach out. I do this when I meditate and ask for guidance and direction. At the time, I was working on a several ideas including *Spiritual Selling* and was not sure which one to work on next.

One of my normal practices is to lookup the name or title of my idea online to see if it is available. When I searched for SpiritualSelling.com the name was taken. Was this a sign to pursue something different?

A few weeks had passed and I was still unsure of my direction. Then I received an email from a guy named Doug I had helped about three years earlier. He was going through a difficult time in his life and had listened to one of my tele-seminars. We spoke for a few hours one evening. Doug was going through a divorce, and had all sorts of issues including plenty of financial troubles. Although he wanted to pay me for my time I felt he needed some kindness and I told him not to worry about it.

I never heard from Doug again until I received the email three years later. He said, *"Hey Joe, I hope all is well. I have been following your work and saw your concept of Spiritual Selling. I was online the other night and saw the name became available so I bought SpiritualSelling.com for you.*" I almost fell off my chair as I read this email. Talk about a validation. Soon after I started the book and attracted a publisher as I outlined earlier.

The interesting thing here was the energy and emotion of this exchange. I had no expectations or thoughts of getting something back for my support. It was just one guy helping a person in need. It was very pure and organic in nature.

This is one of the fascinating things about energy work. We are always sending out and receiving energy. This energy is out there flying around and at the right moment it will align perfectly. You may have had an idea or met someone years earlier and nothing ever came of it. Then one day you reconnect and this old acquaintance can help you with your idea.

In this example, I received this message from the person I helped earlier. In many cases, you will receive your message from a completely different person or source.

SEEING THE BIG PICTURE

As discussed earlier the universe sees your entire life and you only see what is directly in front of you. Is it possible that my helping Doug was all part of a much larger picture? If I could see my entire life I would have known that Doug was going to help me with my *Spiritual Selling* book.

Imagine having the ability to see all the pieces coming together at the perfect time for you. A person you met years earlier reappears to help you, an idea that failed in the past is resurrected to become a huge success, an article you wrote is discovered years later and leads to a big opportunity.

I saw a story about a female entrepreneur. She had written an article for a magazine when she started her business. Not much came of it and she had been struggling to keep the business going. Six years later, an executive came upon the article and contacted her for a major project.

We can't see the future, and that is a good thing. Part of the excitement in life is being surprised when you least expect it. These miracles occur when you are in a state of surrender. At this point your energy is open to receive and you have removed the resistance.

Balance your state of surrender with the actions you take. Make sure you are aligned with your mission and purpose. This is the time when miracles happen.

WHAT IS YOUR INTENTION?

15

L ET'S BEGIN WITH these questions.

Why did you do it?

What do you get out of it?

These are important questions, as they help you gain a deeper understanding of your intentions and desires. Everything we do is driven by a desire. You do something with the intention of getting something. At first blush this may seem negative or selfish to you.

In this case, it is important to go deeper. You may have a desire to help someone in need. Why do you want to help someone while others could care less? At a higher level of awareness, you know when you help another you help yourself. What do you get out of helping someone else? A feeling of love and oneness. That is your desire to help and love others. This is a *pure intention*. You are getting something but that is not why you are doing it.

In a lower state of awareness your intentions will be directed at personal and material gain. You are doing something with the intention of advancing your own agenda. If you help the boss you will receive the promotion you seek. This is a *3D Intention*

(3D for third dimensional or material world). A *3D Intention* is always tied to something here in the physical world. There is a belief that something outside of yourself will make you happy or more successful.

Pure intentions keep you in high energy. You are doing something to feel love, and make the world a better place. There is no expectation or desired outcome. You just do it because it feels good. This is how you feel when you are doing purpose driven work. You may receive love and material success but that is not why you are doing it.

When you are in creation mode and connected to your higher purpose nothing else matters. The creation is the most important thing to you. This moves you into a state of transcendence. The great creators of this world operated in this higher state.

As with all these principles, there can be areas that are not as clear cut. It is very easy to fool yourself. If you are in an approval seeking energy you may help others with the intention of receiving some type of validation or praise. This is an example of a *3D Intention* for personal gain. It seems like you are helping someone, and you may be, but the intention is not pure. You are really doing it for approval or some type of validation.

I noticed this with the volunteers at my son's grammar school. They were mostly women who applied to help with various events and school activities. Many of the meetings were filled with complaints and criticism of the people who did not volunteer. *"She is out playing tennis while I am here doing things for the school"* was a common theme. If these volunteers had a *Pure Intention* their only focus would be helping the school and creating a positive experience for the kids. Instead they judged others, and acted like martyrs.

In life, a desired outcome drives our actions. We do something with the intention of creating a specific result. We may not always create the result we desire but there is always an intention that gets us started.

The big question here is...**Why did you do it?**

We are all designed to do something to get something. Let's take a closer look at your life and why you do the things you do.

Why do you...

» Go to work

» Pay the bills

» Get married

» Have kids

» Buy a home

» Go to the gym

» Go on vacation

There are, of course, practical answers for this list of activities. What happens when you apply the concept of intention?

Why do you go to work? When you are in high energy and aligned with your purpose you are going to make the world a better place. Unfortunately, most people are not going to work for that reason.

If you are not going to do something you love, why would you do it? The obvious answer is to generate an income to pay for what you need. Your intention is to get paid for your work. This is clearly a *3D Intention*. It is connected to your own personal gain and survival. This is not good or bad. We live in a material world and having money is necessary to live here.

What would happen if you began to shift your activities to a

Pure Intention? Every time you do something it is now tied to love and making the world a better place. How would you feel every morning in this state of energy? I know this may seem insane to you right now but I ask you to humor me for the moment.

Adjusting your intention is a mental and emotional shift. You could be doing the exact same thing with a different intention. I know what you are thinking: "Joe I hate my job so this can't work for me."

I tested this theory on myself in the corporate world. My career had stalled and I was moved into a position I did not like. In my state of distress, I decided to look for another job. This went on for several months without success. I was going to work every day to pay the bills and it was draining my energy.

One day I decided to shift my intention. Instead of just going to work to pay the bills I created new programs to help morale and create a better work environment. I had no intention or attachment to the outcome. It was just my way of being more positive and removing myself from the negative energy I was holding.

The staff loved what I was doing, and the energy of the office completely changed. Sales improved and morale soared. It was plain old fun with the intention of making the world, in this case the office, a better place. A few months later I was offered a better position for a lot more money. I wonder if that would have happened if I was still holding the lower negative energy.

You can create miracles in your life by shifting your intentions. As you move to *Pure Intentions* new doors will open and exciting opportunities will appear. Take inventory and evaluate your current intentions. You may be surprised at what you uncover.

RECEIVING WITHOUT EGO

Many people have a real struggle with the concept of receiving. We have been conditioned not to receive and it shows. The poverty, struggle, and pain of the world shows us this reality every day. I am not only speaking of receiving material possessions or money. This all begins with your inability to receive love and kindness.

Everything is energy and energy seeks balance. We are always giving and receiving energy. There are times when we give more and times when we receive more. The goal is to remain balanced and to receive without ego. This can be challenging as you expand your energy and power.

See yourself as Jesus for a moment. He was always operating from a *Pure Intention*. He received a tremendous amount of love and respect. Jesus was held at a high level of esteem by his followers. In this situation, it would very easy to get a big head and lose your way.

You may not see yourself as Jesus and that is a shame. We all carry the unlimited power of the universe within us. As you move to higher energy and awareness you begin to realize this truth.

As a human I ask you to receive love all day long. Do not receive with your ego-self and use it to separate from source. Receive it with grace and know you connected to higher power.

This is easier said than done here in human form. When you begin to receive a lot of love and positive attention it can take you out of your spirit and into your negative-ego.

You may begin to believe you are better than others. We see this with celebrities and the wealthy all the time. This is not a judgment, it is an observation based on how these people are treated.

It is easy to believe you are above others when you are being treated in such a manner. The key here is to receive love, in all forms, and remain connected to your spirit. Know that you are the same as everyone else. There is no difference between the president of a major corporation and the janitor. We are all made up of the same energy and each person should be treated with love and respect.

MOVING INTO CREATION MODE

16

WHEN YOU STOP CHASING you are free to create everything you desire without distraction. Chasing holds you in a negative ego state which blocks your flow of energy. Instead of being in a state of love and pure intention you are in a fear-based condition focused on personal gain.

Now you are free to expand and create your life like never before. There is no telling what amazing things you will create and how you will make the world a better place. The limitations of your mind are removed. Your egoic desires are dissolved and give way to powerful feelings of love-based creation. The greatest creators in the world have worked from this position.

There is only one thing that can derail this ride. Thinking.

Your mind has the power to stop your progress at any time. This is where the disconnect happens for each of us. When you are in pure space you are not thinking. You are flowing and moving with the current. Once your mind gets involved, everything changes. Your mind is logical and wants things to make sense. If it does not make sense to the mind the notion is dismissed.

This creates doubt and fear instead of flow. You have moved from the higher energy of creation to the limiting energy of the third dimension. In physical form, you only see what is in front of you. It is a limited view of the world and universe. In creative flowing energy, there are no obstacles or physical barriers.

Stopping your thought process is easier said than done. As a human, you can never really stop thinking. It is part of who we are and thinking is an important part of life and survival here on earth.

The concept here is to use your mind as a tool, like your computer. You use your computer or cell phone for certain tasks as needed. Many people today have become addicted to technology which engages your mind and removes you from higher energy.

You must work at this non-thinking approach to life. The first step is being aware and understanding how important it is to disconnect from your mind on a regular basis. One of the best ways is meditation. I have been meditating for many years and it has been a tremendous asset. It makes me sad when people tell me they just can't do it.

I am from New York, the noisiest place in the world. If you can meditate in New York, you can do it anywhere. I always talk about meditation at my live events. One evening after a session a guy named Frank approached me regarding meditation. He was a very successful stock broker on Wall Street. Frank was making over a million dollars a year and living the high life. You would think a guy like that would be filled with good energy. He looked exhausted and completely drained when I met him.

Frank hired me to coach him to help with his depression and

feelings of sadness. He was carrying a lot of pain regardless of his success and appearance to the outside world. His mind was going a mile a minute, and I could sense the fractured energy he was carrying.

The first thing I did was talk to him about meditation. He resisted immediately, and told me he could never do it. I insisted and asked him to try it with me for one minute. This is how I get resistant people started, I start with one minute. No one can refuse to try something for one minute. We sat quietly and I took him through some basic breathing and relaxation. When we were finished, he asked me how long we were meditating. I told him it was 10 minutes. His eyes popped out in shock.

Moving forward I helped with his repressed energy and meditation work. Within a month Frank told me he was getting up 20 minutes early every morning to meditate before work. Over time he gained a sense of calmness and peace.

Meditation is nothing more than getting quiet. You do not have to turn it into a big ordeal. Make it a practice to spend some quiet time each day. If you are interested in different types of meditation, there are plenty of books on the subject. I am fan of transcendental meditation, there is also Kundalini, Guided Visualization and many others. Try a few different types and see which one works best for you. Quiet time is when you connect to the infinite wisdom of the universe. Make it a habit. It will serve you well for the rest of your life.

The second step is being aware of your feelings and emotions. This has been a theme throughout this book and I can't emphasize it enough. Your ability to identify and align with your emotions is a very important step.

When your emotions and thoughts are aligned magical things happen in your life. If you ignore and repress your emotions you block your flow and slow things down.

The third step is to allow yourself to feel those emotions as they come up. Do not judge how you feel or make it right or wrong. Your emotions are the gateway to your higher-self and true creative power.

The fourth step is to trust yourself. This is also called going with your gut feeling. In your creative process you will have certain feelings and beliefs. They may go against conventional wisdom but these are the ideas and feelings that change the world.

I am not telling you to live in a vacuum and never accept a suggestion but, if you have strong feelings about your creation trust your gut.

CONNECTING TO YOUR TRUE DESIRE

Your life is a creation and so are you. We come here to create and what we are here to create shows up in the form of desires. You were born with all the skills necessary to fulfill those desires. The highest expression of your life is creation. This happens when you connect to your higher-self and create with pure intention. For many people it takes time to truly connect to your true mission and purpose.

My career was off to rocky start. I did not go to college and started working as a beer delivery man right out of High School. In true chasing form, I purchased a soda delivery business the next year and promptly went bankrupt by age 20.

I bounced around for some time, ended up in advertising, started another business and went bankrupt again. I was now 30 years old and completely lost. In my state of disarray, I decided to go to see a psychologist as my chasing plans were not going very well. I knew something was wrong, but I could not put my finger on it.

I became fascinated with psychology and human behavior. This led me to many books and classes on the subject. Eventually, I moved into metaphysical energy and spiritual work. After a few years of study, I had the desire to share this information with others. I started by speaking at other people's events and to small groups. Then I decided it was time for me to do my own seminar.

This was something I had never done and had no idea how to do it. I enlisted the help of few good friends, and started to move forward. At no point did I think, you have no idea how to do this. I was in creation mode and there was very little thinking in this process, I was focused on what I wanted to create.

One of the principles I learned in my psychology study was the importance of consistent support. A one day seminar would have been nice but I wanted to do something that would be impactful. Having no idea what I was doing I decided to conduct an eight-week program. I felt this was the best way to create the results I desired.

I started running small ads in a local newspaper to get attendees. As I learned in advertising, you always test something before you sell it to the marketplace. This was a free series of sessions for people to attend. All I asked for was their feedback and suggestions.

After months of work and preparation, I was ready. At the time, I was working at a full-time sales job in New York City. The seminars were conducted closer to my home in Queens. I would take the train out of Manhattan, pick up my car and drive to the venue each week. The first night I was very nervous as I was heading over. There were 20 people coming to see me and I was intent on delivering a great experience.

The entire evening was a bit of a blur. The one thing I knew was how great I felt throughout the session. When I got into my car to go home I had an overwhelming feeling. My body felt so full, it was a feeling of contentment, love and complete peace.

As I looked back at this experience I realized there were some key components necessary to create this amazing feeling.

Here they are:

» **I was not attached to the outcome**. There was no concern or attempt to control what was happening or how it would turn out.

» **I had no expectations.** There were no benchmarks for the success of the event.

» **I was not thinking.** This event was created with pure intention. There was no attachment to personal gain or egoic desires.

» **I wanted to help others.** My focus was on sharing the work and helping other people become empowered.

» **There was no fear or worry.** I was a bit anxious about presenting my material but there was no feeling of fear or worry.

» **I was creating based on LOVE!**

Any time I have not been in this state of energy, my results have suffered. I was always chasing the big opportunity, which I thought would bring me the success I desired. This tactic never worked, and always caused more pain and suffering. Attempting to manipulate a situation to create a desired result brings you into lower energy.

YOUR DESIRE IS CODED TO YOUR DNA

I often hear people say, "I do not know what to do." This is what happens when you get stuck in your mind. Your desires are coded into your DNA. You know exactly what you are here to do in this lifetime. The question is, will you allow yourself to do it?

This is where you choose between the safe road or the enlightened path. Most people have been conditioned to select the safe road. When I was a kid all I heard from my grandfather was, *"Get a job in a good company with benefits."* This conditioned belief has been passed down from generation to generation. It is a fear-based belief which keeps you small and weak. There is no bad intention in this advice, it is what people have learned from their parents and passed forward.

Choosing the enlightened path is much more challenging. You are going against your family, society, and conventional wisdom. Your ability to make this choice is made easier or more difficult depending on the type of family you grew up in. For many in my *Baby Boomer* generation, our environments at home were not those of risk and enlightenment. I feel the Millennials are in a much better place in this regard.

I used the word *allow* earlier because that is the key to moving forward. Your mind creates obstacles to stop you from moving forward. You are going to move beyond your mind for the answers and connection you seek. Are you going to *allow* yourself to move forward?

Connecting to your purpose is a simple process. When you allow yourself to connect to your true desire, the doors open and you see everything clearly. The only thing that clogs up the gears is over thinking and worry. Your mind needs the "how to". Your soul does not require this as it knows you have everything you require to complete your mission.

If you are having trouble connecting to your purpose you can download my book *Finding Your Purpose* for FREE at findingyourpurpose.com.

The enlightened path will not be a breeze. There will be many challenges and your resolve will be tested many times. You are sure to encounter many ups and downs as designed by your own karmic journey, the key is to keep moving forward. There will be times when you are ready to give up and walk away. This is when your faith will be tested.

Always go back to your higher-self and stay in a peaceful space. Know that you are always being protected and guided for your highest and greatest good.

YOUR BLUEPRINT FOR SUCCESS AND PEACE

17

I N THIS FINAL CHAPTER, I want to put it all together and give you a snapshot of the processes and concepts I have shared with you. Now is a time to create and share your gifts with the world. This will require work and effort on your part.

In chasing energy, you will feel panic, fear and distress. In peaceful energy, you will feel love and a sense of calmness. Be aware of how you feel and adjust as you go. As humans, we tend to move into negative emotions and fear. The key is being aware and brining yourself back home. Know that the universe is always supporting and protecting you.

Always begin by asking yourself this important question.

Why am I doing this right now?

STEP 1: GETTING OUT OF YOUR MIND

Your mind is a problem-solving machine. It is constantly seeking logical answers, this traps you in a cycle of chasing external desires. The belief is, once you have X you will be happy. When you attain your goal, and the feeling you seek is still missing your mind moves on to the next item.

This is the cycle you are going to break. Stop looking to your mind for an answer that makes sense. You are now moving towards a feeling of peace which is internal, not external. Stop thinking and start feeling.

STEP 2: AWARENESS

Your awareness brings things into your consciousness which gives you the opportunity to make positive changes. This is the beginning of your journey to enlightenment. One of the traps here is to believe once you are aware of something you can control it. This is your ego sending you down a bad road. Do not fall into this trap. Be aware of things from a higher perspective. You are now at the top of the Empire State Building and the view is completely different.

STEP 3: DECISION MAKING

Every day you make a series of decisions based on your feelings and beliefs. Be very aware of how you feel as you make each decision. Ask yourself, is this decision moving me closer to what I desire or further away?

The key here is being honest with how you feel about the decisions you are making. Are you acting out of love or fear? Be sure to make decisions that are aligned with your life and your desires.

Pay attention and chart your energy cycles. This will show you how you are doing and help you make positive adjustments.

Energy Cycle

1. Energy: Everything in your life begins with energy and emotion.

2. Vibration: This emotion creates a vibration of energy.

3. Attraction: The vibration begins to attract people and situations.

4. Outcome: The cycle ends with a result.

This is the fundamental Law of Attraction cycle.

Keep asking yourself...How Do I Feel?

STEP 4: FEEL FIRST, THINK SECOND

Connecting to your emotions is a critical step for your growth. Be aware of your emotions all the time. Move from mental processes to emotional connection. This will take practice before it becomes a habit. The faster you connect to your emotions the faster you will move forward. I suggest an emotional journal. Each night sit down for a few minutes and write down the emotions you experienced that day. This will help heighten your awareness and make you more aware of your emotions.

STEP 5: KNOW YOUR WHY

Before you do something make sure you are aware of why you are doing it. Many of the actions we take are based on unconscious conditioning and feelings of guilt and fear. You must be aware of your emotions and know what is driving your behavior. It is important to be in your heart, not in your head.

Uses these questions:

1. Why am I doing this?

2. Am I in my heart or in my head?

3. Am I creating or controlling?

Your answers to these questions will help you uncover your "why" and put you on the right path.

STEP 6-REMOVE YOUR IDENTITY AND ATTACHMENT TO THE PHYSICAL WORLD

We are here to have an emotional experience in physical form. As you remove the importance of the physical world your energy will elevate to a higher level. Be aware of your feelings and make sure you are not lowering yourself and attaching your value to physical possessions.

These are areas to be aware of:

» Your identity

» Your possessions

» Your position in society

» Your perceived level of power

» Your career

» Your status

You are here to enjoy the physical world. The problems begin when you become attached to possessions and the illusion of power.

STEP 7: ACCEPT YOUR MALCONTENT STATUS

As human beings, we have a strong desire to constantly improve. This is a wonderful trait but it can tie us to the chase in some cases. Honor this trait and embrace your desire to improve. The key here is to accept where you are in life at this moment.

When things do not move as quickly as you would like it is important to step back and relax. There are two options, acceptance and resistance. You may be upset with your current situation or progress, but resisting what is will stop your progress.

Maintain balance with your desire to improve and accept where you are right now. This will help you become more relaxed as you move forward.

STEP 8-CLEAR YOUR NEGATIVE ENERGY

Learning to process your emotions and clear your negative energy is critical to moving your life forward. Every time you deal with your emotions and clear energy you move to a higher level.

Use the processes and meditations in Chapter 5 on a regular basis to accelerate your process and create the life you desire. These are the exercises used to identify and clear your negative energy. Make these exercises part of your daily practice as you move forward.

You will know the energy has been cleared when you can bring up the person or situation without an emotional charge. The negative emotion attached to a certain situation or person will be dissolved.

STEP 9-STOP CHASING THE PAST AND THE FUTURE

Removing time will help you increase the speed at which you move forward. Too many people are chasing an imagined future or holding on to the glory of the past. Time is an illusion we use here in the physical world.

Accept where you are and know you are exactly where you are supposed to be right now. Remain present and enjoy your life in the moment. You may not be where you want to be but you are always moving.

Use the exercises in Chapter 9 to gain clarity and a greater understanding of your attachment to time.

STEP 10-HAVE FAITH

Having faith shifts your energy and creates a completely different feeling. You will not be able to stop chasing without faith. Fear fuels the chase, faith is what ends it. The desire to control people, situations and outcomes is 100% fear-based. Worry is also tied to fear which blocks your flow of energy.

Living in faith is not always easy. Life throws a lot at you and can certainly challenge your faith and trust. When you go off the track be aware and get back on the faith train.

STEP 11-STEP OUT

The more you disconnect from the physical world the higher you go. As your attachment to material items fades, your desire for upset and drama goes away.

When you find yourself in a challenging situation remember to *Step Out*. See yourself floating above the situation and become an observer. Ask yourself, what is really happening here? In this case, you will understand the circumstance at a higher level and know it is an emotional episode. These episodes are designed to help you uncover issues you are here to address.

Never feed the negative energy or drama. Focus on a solution for the greater good and step away. If you are unable to resolve the situation accept this and move on. You will not be able to successfully resolve all issues. I tried for years and it created a lot of pain. There is nothing wrong with accepting this truth. It will help you become more peaceful and understanding.

STEP 12-GO WITH THE FLOW

One of the greatest parts of healing yourself is being in a good flow. When you are flowing, you are not thinking. In this state of being you are allowing yourself to be guided. Take actions that are aligned with your mission and purpose.

Fear, worry and the desire to control takes you out of your flow. Be aware of these feelings and know they are taking you off course. Stay in your flow state and be aware when you veer off track.

STEP 13-THE GREATER GOOD

As my friend Bob the trance-medium said, *"leave the world in better shape than you found it."* You are incredibly powerful and everything you do has an impact on the world.

Make decisions for the *Greater Good* and become a light for others to follow. This is a movement and it is a critical piece of the puzzle as we evolve to a higher place.

STEP 14-SURRENDER

Surrender is not giving up. It is important to let go of your desire to chase. This helps you remove the negative energy and stress that causes so much pain. You must have trust and faith to fully surrender. This is easier said than done.

Know that you are always being guided for your highest and greatest good. Take action when you feel inspired to do so. This will keep you in state of flow.

This is your two-step Surrender process:

Step 1: You mentally agree to let it go (this is the easier step)

Step 2: You let it go emotionally

As you are moving through this process it is a good practice to look for validations. These are messages that confirm your steps along the journey. As your awareness grows your ability to see and understand these messages will be heightened. You can also ask for validations for something specific. This can be done in many ways including meditation and prayer.

STEP 15-KNOW YOUR INTENTION

Your intentions are extremely important as they carry powerful energy. Make sure you are moving forward with pure intentions. Be aware of what is motivating you to act. There are *Pure Intentions* which are love-based and *3D Intentions* which are tied to personal gain and the ego.

It is also important to receive with grace and ease. Remain humble and do not allow your ego to distort your mission or cloud your intentions.

STEP 16-CREATE WITH LOVE

You are here to create and feel love. It sounds so simple but our human journey is designed to create a powerful emotional experience. Accept the fact that you are here to feel joy and pain.

Remain true to yourself and know that your inner guidance is connecting you to your highest self. Be the best version of you and know, as humans we all have our flaws and shortcomings.

Accepting yourself as PERFECT for your journey is the greatest gift you will ever receive.

THE BIG SHIFT

As you stop chasing, your feelings will change. You are still doing things, and moving forward, but the energy is different. Instead of feeling stress and pressure, you feel relaxed and flowing. The daily incidents that triggered you in the past become nothing more than a slight disruption. Things happen, and you will deal with them calmly.

When things are not moving fast enough for your ego, do not stress or push unnecessarily. Take a step back, and know that everything is in divine timing. This is a *Big Shift* and it takes time to become integrated into your system. As time passes, you will become more relaxed in your new state of peace.

MAKING PEACE YOUR HOME

I started doing this work with the idea, or intention, that it would help me become more successful. The concept of peace was sitting in the background. As I continued to clear negative energy my perspective began to change. My attachment to accomplishments and the trappings of the physical world began to fade. Don't get me wrong, it was nice to accomplish something. In the past, it was what I lived for and now it was nice, a very different feeling indeed.

Each day moved me closer to my inner-self and the feeling of peace. I will tell you, when this first started to happen it felt very strange. I had never experienced such a feeling of calmness. When this first started to happen I was ready to jump out of my skin. This is common when you move into different energy. Even though you are moving into higher energy, there will still be feelings of discomfort.

This may sound strange, because you are moving into better, more peaceful energy. With every shift of energy there is an adjustment period. You are moving from one level to the next and it takes time to gain comfort with the new you.

It is like getting a promotion at work. When you are elevated to management status for the first time, it feels strange. You have more responsibility, receive more money, move into a nicer office, and maybe even get an assistant. In the beginning this feels weird. Over time you gain comfort with your new position.

In addition, some people will be happy for you and others may resent you or feel jealous. This also happens when you shift energy. The people around you will feel the change on an unconscious, energetic level. Some will like the new you, and others will not. Each time you elevate, your energy is becoming more powerful. The people who have attempted to control and manipulate you will not like you with more power. Many of these people will be family members and close friends.

The more you love yourself, the higher you go. People who love you will be happy. Those who live in fear will feel threatened. You will find out who truly loves and supports you. Do not judge those who do not support you, as their own fears are holding them back. Accept them and send love knowing they are not aware of what they are doing.

There will always be more challenges to face and emotions to process while you are here on earth. Now you will meet those events in a state of calmness and peace, knowing they are all part of your amazing journey. Process your emotions and allow yourself to have a full experience.

As you elevate yourself you help the world heal. We are all connected and every positive step you take makes the world a better place. Be true to yourself and shine your light on the world.

CPSIA information can be obtained
at www.ICGtesting.com
Printed in the USA
FSOW02n0717180118
43531FS

9 781628 654837